CRY, THE BELOVED COUNTRY

Alan Paton

EDITORIAL DIRECTOR Justin Kestler
MANAGING EDITOR Ben Florman

SERIES EDITORS Boomie Aglietti, Justin Kestler
PRODUCTION Christian Lorentzen

WRITERS Deborah Forbes, Brian Phillips
EDITORS Boomie Aglietti, Thomas Connors

This edition published by Spark Publishing

Spark Publishing
A Division of SparkNotes LLC
120 Fifth Avenue, 8th Floor
New York, NY 10011

01 02 03 04 05 SN 9 8 7 6 5 4 3 2 1

Please send all comments and questions or report errors to
feedback@sparknotes.com.

Library of Congress information available upon request

Printed and bound in the United States

ISBN 1-58663-383-X

INTRODUCTION: STOPPING TO BUY SPARKNOTES ON A SNOWY EVENING

Whose words these are you *think* you know.
Your paper's due tomorrow, though;
We're glad to see you stopping here
To get some help before you go.

Lost your course? You'll find it here.
Face tests and essays without fear.
Between the words, good grades at stake:
Get great results throughout the year.

Once school bells caused your heart to quake
As teachers circled each mistake.
Use SparkNotes and no longer weep,
Ace every single test you take.

Yes, books are lovely, dark, and deep,
But only what you grasp you keep,
With hours to go before you sleep,
With hours to go before you sleep.

Contents

CONTEXT

ALAN PATON WAS BORN in the South African city of Pietermaritzburg on January 11, 1903, to a Scottish father and a South African mother of English heritage. An active and intelligent child, Paton went on to attend Natal University, where, among other activities, he wrote poetry and served as student body president. At the age of twenty-two, he became a teacher at two of South Africa's elite, all-white schools, first in the village of Ixopo, then in Pietermaritzburg. Ten years later, he left teaching to pursue a career as a reformatory worker. He was appointed principal of the Diepkloof Reformatory, a prison school for black youths. While at the reformatory, Paton attempted to loosen the restrictions placed on the youths and emphasized preparation for life outside the reformatory walls. He also traveled extensively to study reformatory schools worldwide. It was on one such trip, shortly after World War II, that he wrote *Cry, the Beloved Country,* the novel that earned him his fame as an author.

Cry, the Beloved Country was published in 1948 to overwhelming international acclaim—at the time of the author's death, in 1988, more than fifteen million copies of the novel had been sold, and it had been published in twenty different languages. In Paton's native South Africa, however, praise for *Cry, the Beloved Country* remained muted, and the novel's objective take on the problems of racial inequality in South Africa created much controversy. Nonetheless, Paton's reputation as one of South Africa's greatest writers remained secure, though his subsequent novels, *Too Late the Phalarope* (1953) and *Ah, But Your Land Is Beautiful* (1981), were praised by critics but failed to generate the same excitement as *Cry, the Beloved Country.*

Although apartheid, South Africa's infamous system of enforced racial segregation, was not instituted until after the novel's publication, the South Africa of *Cry, the Beloved Country* was nevertheless suffering from the effects of racial segregation, enforced inequality, and prejudice. The crime rate was high, and attacks on whites by black agitators caused panic among the country's white citizens. Black South Africans found themselves adrift as the traditional tribal cultures gave way to the lure of the cities, and many South

Africans were left without any moral or social organization to turn to. Whites held a monopoly on political power, and they did nothing to alleviate the extreme poverty among black South Africans, which in turn led many young black men to crime. The gold mines, which were so vital to South Africa's economy, depended on cheap black labor to remain profitable, and as a result, the workers were paid barely enough to survive. But those in power inevitably broke up attempts to strike or seek a better wage.

Cry, the Beloved Country is set in this tense and fragile society, where the breathtaking beauty of the nation's natural landscape is tainted by the fears of its people. And yet, the message of the novel is one of hope. Characters such as Stephen Kumalo, James Jarvis, and Theophilus Msimangu reveal a potential for goodness in humankind, and are able to defuse hatred, overcome fear, and take the first steps necessary for mending a broken nation.

HISTORICAL BACKGROUND

Cry, the Beloved Country is set in South Africa in the 1940s. Its story unfolds against a backdrop of economic and political tensions that have a lengthy, complicated history. Thousands of years before the first Europeans arrived, southern Africa was populated by various African tribal groups, including the San, the Khoikhoi, and, later on, Bantu-speaking peoples who were ancestors of the modern Zulus. The first European settlers in South Africa, the Dutch, arrived in the mid-1600s. The Dutch wanted only to set up bases for trade, not to colonize the country, and they met with little resistance. But by the mid-1700s, the Dutch, who had come to be known as the Boers and who had developed their own language, Afrikaans, had begun to settle deeper and deeper into the country. In a process similar to the displacement and destruction of Native American life in the United States, African tribes were forced off their traditional lands, decimated by disease, and defeated in battles against the well-armed Boers.

English settlers first arrived in 1795. Unlike the Dutch, by the early 1800s the English decided to make South Africa a full-fledged colony. Concentrated in coastal cities, the English soon found themselves in conflict with Boer farmers, who called themselves "the white tribe of Africa." The Boers moved north, away from the coast, while the Zulus, led by the famous warrior-leader Shaka, pressed south on a military campaign. Inevitably, the two groups clashed, fighting a number of bloody battles before the Zulus were defeated. The Boers created several independent republics, but when diamonds and gold were discovered in the Boer territories, the British moved to annex them, leading to the first Anglo-Boer war in 1881. The Boers regained the independence of their territories, but when gold was discovered near what is now Johannesburg in 1886, the British invaded the area again. The second Anglo-Boer war lasted from 1899 to 1902. The victorious British were able to establish rule, and they officially established the Union of South Africa in 1910.

Cry, the Beloved Country takes place after these upheavals and immediately before the implementation, in 1948, of apartheid, which codified the systematic inequalities depicted in the novel. During the time in which the novel is set, black workers were permitted to hold only unskilled jobs and were subject to "pass laws" that restricted their freedom of movement. In 1913, the Natives Land Act radically limited the amount of land that black South Africans were permitted to own. As the character Arthur Jarvis states in the novel, just one-tenth of the land was set aside for four-fifths of the country's people. The resultant overcrowding led many black South Africans to migrate to Johannesburg to work in the mines. Those in power welcomed the influx of cheap labor but failed to provide adequate housing or services to address the mass migration. These are the circumstances under which the character Stephen Kumalo leaves his impoverished rural village to search for his son in Johannesburg.

Though Paton's novel helped raise the social consciousness of white South Africa, things got much worse before they got better. In 1948, the National Party (representing Afrikaner and conservative interests) gained power and introduced apartheid. Under apartheid, every South African was classified according to race, and the Group Areas Act enforced the physical separation of blacks from whites. Every aspect of South African life was racially segregated. Under the leadership of Nelson Mandela, the African National Congress (ANC), which had been founded in 1912 as the South African Native National Congress and renamed in 1923, began protests against the new laws in the form of strikes and marches. After decades of struggle and bloodshed, the ANC prevailed, and South Africa held its first free election in 1994. Mandela was elected president, apartheid was dismantled, and the country ratified one of the most liberal constitutions in the world.

PLOT OVERVIEW

I N THE REMOTE VILLAGE OF NDOTSHENI, in the Natal province of eastern South Africa, the Reverend Stephen Kumalo receives a letter from a fellow minister summoning him to Johannesburg, a city in South Africa. He is needed there, the letter says, to help his sister, Gertrude, who the letter says has fallen ill. Kumalo undertakes the difficult and expensive journey to the city in the hopes of aiding Gertrude and of finding his son, Absalom, who traveled to Johannesburg from Ndotsheni and never returned. In Johannesburg, Kumalo is warmly welcomed by Msimangu, the priest who sent him the letter, and given comfortable lodging by Mrs. Lithebe, a Christian woman who feels that helping others is her duty. Kumalo visits Gertrude, who is now a prostitute and liquor-seller, and persuades her to come back to Ndotsheni with her young son.

A more difficult quest follows when Kumalo and Msimangu begin searching the labyrinthine metropolis of Johannesburg for Absalom. They visit Kumalo's brother, John, who has become a successful businessman and politician, and he directs them to the factory where his son and Absalom once worked together. One clue leads to another, and as Kumalo travels from place to place, he begins to see the gaping racial and economic divisions that are threatening to split his country. Eventually, Kumalo discovers that his son has spent time in a reformatory and that he has gotten a girl pregnant.

Meanwhile, the newspapers announce that Arthur Jarvis, a prominent white crusader for racial justice, has been murdered in his home by a gang of burglars. Kumalo and Msimangu learn that the police are looking for Absalom, and Kumalo's worst suspicions are confirmed when Absalom is arrested for Jarvis's murder. Absalom has confessed to the crime, but he claims that two others, including John Kumalo's son, Matthew, aided him and that he did not intend to murder Jarvis. With the help of friends, Kumalo obtains a lawyer for Absalom and attempts to understand what his son has become. John, however, makes arrangements for his own son's defense, even though this split will worsen Absalom's case. When Kumalo tells Absalom's pregnant girlfriend what has happened, she is saddened by the news, but she joyfully agrees to his proposal that she marry his son and return to Ndotsheni as Kumalo's daughter-in-law.

Meanwhile, in the hills above Ndotsheni, Arthur Jarvis's father, James Jarvis, tends his bountiful land and hopes for rain. The local police bring him news of his son's death, and he leaves immediately for Johannesburg with his wife. In an attempt to come to terms with what has happened, Jarvis reads his son's articles and speeches on social inequality and begins a radical reconsideration of his own prejudices. He and Kumalo meet for the first time by accident, and after Kumalo has recovered from his shock, he expresses sadness and regret for Jarvis's loss. Both men attend Absalom's trial, a fairly straightforward process that ends with the death penalty for Absalom and an acquittal for his co-conspirators. Kumalo arranges for Absalom to marry the girl who bears his child, and they bid farewell. The morning of his departure, Kumalo rouses his new family to bring them back to Ndotsheni only to find that Gertrude has disappeared and run back to her old life of sin.

Kumalo is now deeply aware of how his people have lost the tribal structure that once held them together, and he returns to his village troubled by the situation. It turns out that James Jarvis has been having similar thoughts. Arthur Jarvis's young son befriends Kumalo, and as the young boy and the old man become acquainted, James Jarvis becomes increasingly involved with helping the struggling village. He donates milk at first, then makes plans for a dam and hires an agricultural expert to demonstrate newer, less devastating farming techniques. When Jarvis's wife dies, Kumalo and his congregation send a wreath to express their sympathy. Just as the diocese's bishop is on the verge of transferring Kumalo, Jarvis sends a note of thanks for the wreath and offers to build the congregation a new church, and Kumalo is permitted to stay in his parish.

On the evening before his son's execution, Kumalo goes into the mountains to await the appointed time in solitude. On the way, he encounters Jarvis, and the two men speak of the village, of lost sons, and of Jarvis's bright young grandson, whose innocence and honesty have impressed both men. When Kumalo is alone, he weeps for his son's death and clasps his hands in prayer as dawn breaks over the valley.

CHARACTER LIST

Stephen Kumalo One of the novel's two protagonists. Kumalo is an elderly Zulu priest who has spent all of his life in the village of Ndotsheni. He is a quiet, humble, and gentle man with a strong moral sense and an abiding faith in God. He is not perfect, however, and occasionally gives in to the temptation to hurt others with harsh words or lies. The dignity and grace with which he accepts his suffering, however, along with his determination to help his people in spite of his limitations, make him the moral center of the novel.

James Jarvis The novel's other protagonist, awhite landowner whose farm overlooks Ndotsheni. When he first appears in the novel, Jarvis is a relatively conservative farmer and a man of few words. But the tragic news that his only son, Arthur, has been murdered leads him to Johannesburg, where he begins to rethink his opinions and his relationship to the villagers that live below his farm.

Theophilus Msimangu Stephen Kumalo's host and guide in Johannesburg. A tall, young minister at the Mission House in Sophiatown, Msimangu has an acute understanding of the problems that face South Africa. He helps Kumalo understand the people and places that they encounter, and is unfailingly sympathetic to Kumalo, making Kumalo's quest his top priority. He sometimes speaks unkindly, but he quickly repents. His eventual decision to enter a monastery is a final testament to the depth of his faith and generosity.

Absalom Kumalo Stephen Kumalo's son. After fleeing home for Johannesburg, Absalom quickly goes astray, but even after he commits murder, he is able to reclaim his fundamental decency. His decision to move to Johannesburg is part of a larger trend of young black people fleeing their villages for the cities. Absalom's story is a cautionary tale of the dangers of this movement. Seeming to lack a reliable moral compass, he is influenced by bad companions and begins a criminal career.

John Kumalo Stephen Kumalo's brother. Formerly a humble carpenter and a practicing Christian, John Kumalo becomes a successful businessman and one of the three most powerful black politicians in Johannesburg. He has a beautiful and powerful voice, which he uses to speak out for the rights of black South Africans, but his fear of punishment prevents him from pushing for actual radical change, and he is considered by many to be without courage.

Arthur Jarvis Arthur Jarvis's name first appears in the novel after he has been murdered, but he is a powerful presence whose legacy hovers over the whole novel. An engineer and fierce advocate for justice for black South Africans, he is shot dead in his home by Absalom Kumalo.

Mrs. Kumalo Stephen Kumalo's strong-minded, supportive, and loving wife. Mrs. Kumalo and her husband make household decisions as equals, and she bears hardship gracefully. When Kumalo is inclined to brood, she rouses him to action, and it is she who supplies the courage needed to read the bad news that the mail brings from Johannesburg.

Gertrude Kumalo Stephen Kumalo's sister and the original reason for his trip to Johannesburg. Gertrude, twenty-five years younger than Kumalo and living in Johannesburg, is easily influenced. When Kumalo reminds her of her Christian duties and obligations, she attempts to return to them, but she lacks real determination. Although she considers joining a convent, she eventually succumbs to her original impulses and returns to her life of crime.

Gertrude's son Kumalo's nephew. He brings comfort to Kumalo during his troubles. He returns with Kumalo to Ndotsheni, where Absalom's wife raises him.

Mrs. Lithebe The woman with whom Kumalo stays in Johannesburg. Mrs. Lithebe is an Msutu woman who lives in Sophiatown and takes in boarders, especially priests. She is a good and generous Christian who believes that helping others is simply her duty.

The young man A young white man who works at the reformatory and attempts to reform Absalom. Although he does, on one occasion, chastise Kumalo, he does so because he cares much for his pupils, and the thought of Absalom's predicament pains him.

Father Vincent An Anglican priest from England who stays at the Sophiatown Mission and offers to help Kumalo with his troubles. Father Vincent counsels Kumalo when he is brokenhearted over his son and presides over the wedding between Absalom and Absalom's girlfriend. He is warm and understanding, and he possesses deep faith.

Absalom's girlfriend The kindhearted and quiet sixteen-year-old girl whom Absalom has impregnated. She has run away from her dysfunctional family but still seeks a family structure and bonds. She is sexually experienced but essentially innocent, obedient, and grateful for adult protection.

Margaret Jarvis James Jarvis's wife. Margaret takes the death of her son very hard. She is a physically fragile and loving woman who commiserates with and supports her husband through their grief. She also shares in his plans to help Ndotsheni.

CHARACTER LIST

John Harrison The brother of Mary Jarvis, Arthur Jarvis's wife. John is young and quick-witted, and shares Arthur's opinions about the rights of the black population in South Africa. He provides companionship to James Jarvis in Johannesburg.

Mr. Harrison Mary Jarvis's father. Mr. Harrison has conservative political views and blames black South Africans for the country's problems. Though he disagrees with Arthur, he admires Arthur's courage.

Arthur's son Although only a child, Arthur's son is very much like his father. He is curious, intelligent, and generous. He treats black people with unusual courtesy and pleases Kumalo by visiting him and practicing Zulu.

Napoleon Letsitsi The agricultural expert hired by James Jarvis to teach better farming techniques to the people of Ndotsheni. A well-educated middle-class black man, Letsitsi earns a good salary and is eager to help build his country. Although grateful for the help of good white men, he nonetheless looks forward to an Africa in which black people will not rely on whites for their basic needs.

Matthew Kumalo John Kumalo's son. We learn little about Matthew, but he is important to the plot of the novel, as he is a good friend and eventual accomplice of Absalom's. Eventually, however, Matthew denies having been present at the robbery, turning his back on his cousin and friend.

Johannes Pafuri The third young man present at the attempted robbery of Arthur Jarvis's house. According to Absalom's testimony, Pafuri is the ringleader of the group, deciding the time of the robbery and having his weapon "blessed" to give them good luck.

Mr. Carmichael An acquaintance of Father Vincent's who becomes Absalom's lawyer. Mr. Carmichael is a tall and serious man who carries himself with an almost royal bearing. He takes Absalom's case *pro deo* ("for God").

The Judge The Judge who presides over Absalom's case seems to be a fair-minded man, but he is constrained by unjust laws and applies them strictly.

Dubula The second in a trio of powerful black politicians in Johannesburg. Dubula provides the heart to complement John Kumalo's voice. The bus boycott and the construction of Shanty Town are his handiwork.

Tomlinson The third colleague of Dubula and John Kumalo. While not a great orator, Tomlinson is considered the smartest of the three.

Mary Jarvis Arthur Jarvis's wife. Mary takes her husband's murder hard, but she remains strong for her children. She shares her husband's commitment to justice.

ANALYSIS OF MAJOR CHARACTERS

STEPHEN KUMALO

Stephen Kumalo is the protagonist and moral compass of *Cry, the Beloved Country.* He is a quiet, humble man, with a strong faith in God and a clear sense of right and wrong. An Anglican priest, Kumalo cares for his parishioners and presides over the modest church of the village he calls home. By village standards, Kumalo and his wife are middle-class, living in a house with several rooms. They struggle, however, to save money for their son's schooling and for a new stove. Kumalo is not flawless, and he occasionally erupts in anger and tells lies. Praying to God, however, saves him from temptation, and he always repents when he speaks unfairly.

As the novel begins, Kumalo undertakes his first journey to the city of Johannesburg. He is intimidated and overwhelmed by the city, betraying his simple background. With the help of generous hosts, however, he is able to put his fear aside and search with determination for his son. As the search drags on, we become aware of Kumalo's physical weaknesses—according to African tradition, he has reached the time in his life when his children should be caring for him. He is forced instead to search for his son. When it becomes clear that Absalom is in grave trouble, Kumalo's body is further broken by his grief. His faith wavers, too, but he seeks the help of friends in the ministry, who support him and pray with him. By the time Kumalo leaves Johannesburg, he is deeply sad, but his faith is buoyed by the generosity of others. When he returns to his village, Kumalo works to improve the lives of his parishioners. In the end, he faces his son's death with mourning, but also with a sense of peace.

JAMES JARVIS

James Jarvis undergoes a journey parallel to that of Kumalo, although he is never granted the chance to be reunited with his son, Arthur, physically. Jarvis is a white, English-speaking farmer who lives on a hill above Ndotsheni. When the novel begins, Jarvis is ignorant of or indifferent to the injustices of South Africa. He cares for his farm and his family, and he more or less takes for granted the political system in which he lives. Jarvis's complacency is shattered when he learns that his son has been killed. He goes to stay with his son's in-laws, the Harrisons, in Johannesburg, where he learns that Arthur had become a leader in the community, valued by people from all racial groups for his speeches on social justice. Jarvis here realizes that his son had become a stranger to him.

In an effort to understand his son better, Jarvis reads Arthur's writings about the injustices he perceives in South Africa, and he is moved by his son's language and ideas. Jarvis does not undergo a political conversion so much as a moral one—he is not interested, for example, by John Kumalo's speech before the strike at the mines. Once he returns to Ndotsheni, however, he works hard to make things better for the people of the village. He donates milk to the young children and arranges to have a dam built to irrigate the soil better. Additionally, he hires an agricultural expert to teach the farmers to preserve the soil. When he suffers from a second tragedy—the death of his wife—he consoles himself by carrying out his wife's wish that he build a new church for the community. Jarvis's efforts require personal sacrifices, as it costs him both money and the respect of many of his peers. It is clear, however, that he has made a firm commitment to the villagers, and, though he is a man of few words, he expresses himself beautifully through his actions.

THEOPHILUS MSIMANGU

Msimangu is warm, generous, and humble young minister in Sophiatown. He guides both Kumalo and us through Johannesburg, explaining the political and socioeconomic difficulties that the black population faces and providing shrewd commentary on both blacks and whites. He assists Kumalo with great sensitivity, working to spare him pain when he can and arranging time for him to rest. In general, he makes Kumalo's time in Johannesburg bearable.

Of all the characters in the novel, Msimangu has the clearest understanding of South Africa's injustices, and he serves as Paton's mouthpiece in suggesting a solution: Christian love. According to Msimangu, white South Africans oppress the blacks because they fear their numbers and their power. Msimangu believes that only selfless love can counter this fear. Msimangu's own selflessness is affirmed at the novel's close, when he gives his worldly possessions to Kumalo and joins a monastery.

ABSALOM KUMALO

Though Absalom is at the center of the plot of *Cry, the Beloved Country,* he is a somewhat mysterious figure. Having left home like most of the young people of Ndotsheni, Absalom finds work in Johannesburg. For reasons that are never made clear, however, he loses touch with his family and falls into a life of crime. Young and impressionable, Absalom carries a gun for protection, but when he fires the weapon in fear, he ends up killing Arthur Jarvis. Absalom's basic innocence is affirmed when he confesses everything to the police, and even they seem to suspect his friend Johannes and not him for the murder. Nonetheless, the court holds Absalom solely responsible for the crime. He tries to communicate honestly with Kumalo, though no words can explain what he has done. Originally afraid to die, Absalom appears to reconcile himself to his impending execution and writes respectfully to his mother and father until the time of his death, demonstrating a newfound maturity that allows him to approach death gracefully.

ARTHUR JARVIS

Arthur Jarvis is murdered before we even hear of him, but his writings provide him with the opportunity to speak for himself. A staunch opponent of South Africa's racial injustices, Arthur Jarvis spent his life at the center of the debates on racism and poverty, and his essays and articles provide answers to many of the novel's questions. His motives are selfless; he works for change not because he seeks personal glory but because he is weary of the system's contradictions and oppression. As much as Msimangu, Arthur Jarvis is the solution South Africa needs, and although he is murdered, some hope lives on in his young son.

CHARACTER ANALYSIS

THEMES, MOTIFS & SYMBOLS

THEMES

Themes are the fundamental and often universal ideas explored in a literary work.

RECONCILIATION BETWEEN FATHERS AND SONS

Cry, the Beloved Country chronicles the searches of two fathers for their sons. For Kumalo, the search begins as a physical one, and he spends a number of days combing Johannesburg in search of Absalom. Although most of his stops yield only the faintest clues as to Absalom's whereabouts, the clues present a constantly evolving picture of who Absalom has become. As Kumalo knocks on the doors of Johannesburg's slums, he hears of his son's change from factory worker to burglar, then from promising reformatory pupil to killer. When Kumalo and Absalom are finally reunited after Absalom's incarceration, they are virtual strangers to each other. The ordeal of the trial brings them closer together, but it is not until after the guilty verdict that Kumalo begins to understand Absalom. In Absalom's letters from prison, Kumalo finds evidence of true repentance and familiar flashes of the little boy he remembers.

Jarvis has no actual searching to do, but it takes him little time to realize that he knows little about his own son. Away from Ndotsheni, Arthur has become a tireless advocate for South Africa's black population, an issue on which he and his father have not always agreed. Reconciliation with a dead man might seem an impossible task, but Jarvis finds the necessary materials in Arthur's writings, which give Jarvis clear and succinct insights into the man that Arthur had become, and even instill in Jarvis a sense of pride.

THE VICIOUS CYCLE OF INEQUALITY AND INJUSTICE

Kumalo's search for his son takes place against the backdrop of massive social inequalities, which, if not directly responsible for Absalom's troubles, are certainly catalysts for them. Because black South Africans are allowed to own only limited quantities of land, the natural resources of these areas are sorely taxed. The soil of Ndotsheni turns on its inhabitants—exhausted by over-planting and over-grazing, the land becomes sharp and hostile. For this reason, most young people leave the villages to seek work in the cities. Both Gertrude and Absalom find themselves caught up in this wave of emigration, but the economic lure of Johannesburg leads to danger. Facing limited opportunities and disconnected from their family and tribal traditions, both Gertrude and Absalom turn to crime.

Gertrude's and Absalom's stories recur on a large scale in Johannesburg, and the result is a city with slum neighborhoods and black gangs that direct their wrath against whites. In search of quick riches, the poor burglarize white homes and terrorize their occupants. The white population then becomes paranoid, and the little sympathy they do have for problems such as poor mine conditions disappears. Blacks find themselves subjected to even more injustice, and the cycle spirals downward. Both sides explain their actions as responses to violence from the other side. Absalom's lawyer, for instance, claims that Absalom is society's victim, and white homeowners gather government troops to counter what they see as a rising menace. There is precious little understanding on either side, and it seems that the cycle of inequality and injustice will go on endlessly.

CHRISTIANITY AND INJUSTICE

In the tremendous hardships that Kumalo faces, his main solace comes from his faith in God. When he finds out what has happened to his son, his faith is shaken but not broken, and he turns to his fellow priests for comfort. Much of Kumalo's time is spent in prayer, both for the souls lost in Johannesburg and for the fractured society of his village. Not just a form of comfort, Christianity proves to be a tool for resisting oppressive authority as well. Arthur Jarvis's final essay, for example, calls the policies of South Africa's mine un-Christian. Some allusions are made as well to the priests who have made social justice in South Africa their leading cause. As demonstrated with Msimangu, religion is often held up as South Africa's only possible means of avoiding the explosion of its racial tensions.

Christianity is also, however, associated with injustice. John Kumalo reminds his brother that black priests are paid less than white ones, and argues that the church works against social change by reconciling its members to their suffering. He paints an infuriating picture of a bishop who condemns injustice while living in the luxury that such injustice provides. At the same time as he calls the policies of the mines un-Christian, Arthur Jarvis states that these policies have long been justified through faulty Christian reasoning. Arthur Jarvis mentions that some people argue that God meant for blacks to be unskilled laborers and that it is thus wrong to provide opportunities for improvement and education. The novel frequently explores the idea that in the wrong hands, Christianity can put a needy population to sleep or lend legitimacy to oppressive ideas.

MOTIFS

Motifs are recurring structures, contrasts, or literary devices that can help to develop and inform the text's major themes.

DESCRIPTIONS OF NATURE
The novel's descriptions of the beauty of Natal highlight the contrast between the various ways of life in South Africa. The hills and rivers of white farmland are always depicted as being fruitful and lovely, but the land of the black farmers is always shown as barren, dry, and hostile. This contrast between the natural beauty of South Africa and the ugliness brought on by its politics shows the necessity of change. It also, however, offers some hope. The land may be ravaged, but it is clearly not naturally infertile. With the right nurturing and protection, the potential for real beauty seems endless.

REPENTANCE
Throughout the novel, a number of characters lash out in anger. Msimangu speaks harshly when he learns that Absalom has abandoned his girlfriend, the young man from the reformatory speaks harshly when he is disappointed in Absalom, and Kumalo gets upset, at various times, with his wife, his son's girlfriend, and his brother. Often, these episodes are truly ugly. When the young man whirls on Kumalo, for example, his anger is made even uglier by Kumalo's fragile helplessness. Similarly, when Kumalo cruelly asks Absalom's girlfriend if she will be his lover, the combination of lechery and bullying is unappealing.

Even acts as vile as these, however, can be atoned for by sincere repentance. Although the characters lash out in anger, their repentance is always met with forgiveness, and even the gravest insults are excused. This pattern demonstrates the power of caring to overcome bitterness. Social relationships are torn by anger, but they can be mended with kindness.

REPEATED PHRASES

A number of phrases are repeated throughout the novel, and they show subtle changes in meaning every time they appear. One such phrase is "as was the custom" or "it was not the custom." Kumalo expects to be treated as an inferior by white people in small, customary ways. When these customs are violated, the concessions seem to be minor, but the repetition of the phrase alerts us as to how often these small acts of defiance occur. The seriousness of these actions is summed up in the phrase "not a thing to be done lightly," which also appears with some frequency. Instances of reconciliation are often so nuanced in the novel that we can easily miss their significance and think that Kumalo's and Jarvis's efforts have all been for nothing. With the recurrence of the phrase "not a thing to be done lightly," however, it becomes clearer that taboos are being broken more and more and that blacks and whites are inching closer to change.

SYMBOLS

Symbols are objects, characters, figures, or colors used to represent abstract ideas or concepts.

THE CHURCH

The church in Ndotsheni is a simple, rough structure that represents a faith that is humble and unpretentious. With its leaky roof, the church seems to offer little shelter from the elements, but confirmations and other ceremonies occur there nonetheless—with nothing better available, the congregation must simply make do.

Although it is a house of God, the church is also closely linked to Kumalo. It is introduced to us almost as an extension of his house, and it is he who decides when services will be held and does its accounting. When Kumalo returns from Johannesburg, it becomes apparent that his young successor has had no success in making the church his own, and that both the building and its flock are fundamentally Kumalo's. Jarvis's offer to build a new church for the community is a symbol not only of his commitment to Ndotsheni but also of his new friendship with Kumalo.

BRIGHTNESS

Both Arthur and his son are notable for their "brightness," a symbol of their eager intellects and generous hearts. Although they don't shine physically, there is still something inherently brilliant about them that holds unquestionable promise. The novel's mystical way of describing them is strongly reminiscent of the language typically used to describe angels, messengers of God who take human form but are somehow obviously more than human. The character of Arthur's son seems to be especially developed as an almost divine agent. He rides around Ndotsheni on his horse, appearing periodically to raise Kumalo's spirits, and his visits are occasionally followed by some generosity from his grandfather (an unexpected milk delivery, for example, or the arrival of Napoleon Letsitsi). Both Arthur and his son, then, help to bring good to their fellow men.

Summary & Analysis

Book I: Chapters 1–3

Summary — Chapter 1

In the hilly South African province of Natal, a lovely road winds its way up from the village of Ixopo to Carisbrooke, a journey of seven miles. This misty vantage point looks out over one of the fairest valleys of Africa, where the native birds sing and the grass is dense and green. The lush grass of the hills clings to the rain and mist, soaking up the moisture, which in turn feeds every stream. Although cattle graze here, their feeding has not destroyed the land, and the few fires that burn have not harmed the soil. As the hills roll down to the valley below, however, they become red and bare. The grass there has been destroyed by cattle and fire, and the streams have all run dry. When storms come, the red dirt runs like blood, and the crops are withered and puny. These valleys are the homes of the elderly, who scrape at the dirt for sustenance. Some mothers live here with their children, but all the able-bodied young people have long since moved away.

Summary — Chapter 2

The Reverend Stephen Kumalo, a native Zulu, sits in his house writing when a young girl appears with a letter. After sending the girl to the kitchen for some food, Kumalo wonders who may have sent the letter. It is from Johannesburg, but so many members of his family have been in the city for so long without word that it could be from any of them, and he cannot recognize the handwriting. Among others, Kumalo's brother, John, lives in Johannesburg, as does their sister Gertrude, who is twenty-five years younger than Kumalo, and Kumalo's son, Absalom, who went to the city in search of Gertrude and has never returned.

Apprehensive, Kumalo calls to his wife, who confirms that the letter is not from their son. Finally, Kumalo's wife musters the courage to open the letter and reads it aloud in faltering English. It is from a minister in Johannesburg named Theophilus Msimangu, who reports that Gertrude is ill and who requests that Kumalo come to the Sophiatown section of Johannesburg.

23

Kumalo's wife asks what Kumalo intends to do, and he reluctantly tells her to bring him the money they have saved for Absalom's education at St. Chad's, the local school. Kumalo's resolve falters when he holds the money in his hand, but his wife comments that there is no longer any point in saving it—Absalom has gone to Johannesburg, and those who go there do not return. Kumalo reacts angrily to his wife's suggestion that their son will never come back, and although she protests, saying that Kumalo is hurting himself, he continues to deny her claim angrily. When he realizes that his words are wounding his wife, however, Kumalo calms down and reconciles himself to the inevitable. He and his wife pool the St. Chad's money with the rest of their savings, resignedly giving up the money they intended to spend on clothes and a new stove. Kumalo apologizes humbly to his wife for his unkindness, then heads off to his church to pray for guidance and forgiveness. His wife watches him through the window with a weariness born from years of suffering.

SUMMARY — CHAPTER 3

Kumalo waits for the Johannesburg train at Carisbrooke. Generally, this journey is shrouded in mist, which some find to be an ominous sign and others find a mysterious prelude to adventure. Kumalo, however, pays little attention to his surroundings. He is anxious about his sister's health, the potential costs of treating her illness, and the chaos of Johannesburg, where there are many buses and one can be killed just by crossing the street, as happened to a twelve-year-old boy who was an acquaintance of Kumalo's. His gravest concern is his son.

The train arrives, and Kumalo bids farewell to the companion who has helped him bring his bags to the station. As Kumalo boards the train, his companion passes on a request from a man named Sibeko, whose daughter accompanied a white family to Johannesburg and has not written since. Kumalo says he will do what he can. He boards one of the train's designated non-European carriages, where he searches in vain for a fellow passenger of the same social class as himself. He then goes to the window to say farewell to his friend and asks why Sibeko couldn't make his request himself. His companion explains that Sibeko does not belong to Kumalo's church, but Kumalo proclaims that they are all of the same people and should not hesitate to go to one another in times of trouble. He states grandiosely that he will check on

Sibeko's daughter, although he will be busy, as he always is when he is in Johannesburg. Since Kumalo has never been to Johannesburg before, this statement is a fib, but it has the desired effect of impressing Kumalo's fellow passengers.

Once the train leaves the station, however, Kumalo's old fears return. He worries about the city, about the fate of his family members, particularly his son, and about his intuition that he "lives in a world not made for him." As the train rattles along toward Johannesburg, Kumalo takes refuge in his Bible, the only thing that brings him comfort in these troubled times.

ANALYSIS — BOOK I: CHAPTERS 1–3

The opening chapters of *Cry, The Beloved Country* are built on a series of contrasts that underscore the sharp divisions plaguing South Africa. The most immediate and stark contrast is that between Natal's lush hills and its barren valley, a contrast that plays out in the different ways the landscape affects the inhabitants' lives. The different aesthetic qualities of these two areas reflect these areas' differing abilities to be productive for their people. The grass of the hills is pleasing to bare feet, but even more important, it traps moisture and ensures that the soil will remain rich. In contrast, the coarse, ravaged land of the valley settlements is not only ugly, but can barely support human life.

The sharp contrasts in the landscape also underscore the unfairness and self-destructiveness of a segregated society. Although the first chapters of the novel do not make it explicit, the ugliness of the land is a result of the segregation policy pursued by the white rulers. White farms are symbolically located at the tops of the hills, where the land is green and fruitful. Black South Africans, however, are forced to tend their settlements at the bottom of the hills, in the unforgiving land of the valley. Overcrowding leads to over-grazing and over-farming, a vicious cycle that lessens the land's productivity each year. Left to its own devices, Paton suggests, the earth is nurturing and benevolent, as can be seen in the prosperous areas. When subjected to the effects of segregation, however, the earth becomes cruel, barren, and uncooperative toward its tenants.

Another contrast exists between the comfortable dignity of Kumalo's rural life and the urban chaos that is beginning to encroach upon it. In Natal, Kumalo's life is orderly. His village holds him in high esteem, and the child who brings him his letter is awed by the comforts of his home. With the arrival of Msimangu's letter from the city, however, comes discord. Until that moment, Kumalo and his wife have lived in relative harmony, and their careful budgeting and saving shows their organization and cooperation. The arrival of the letter, however, stands this simple order on its head, as Kumalo and his wife argue and are forced to squander their savings. In the station and among the simple country folk on the train, Kumalo is master of his domain, but every time he thinks of the city and its dangers, he becomes small and weak, an old man.

Kumalo's numerous moments of weakness in the novel's early chapters make him a more compelling character. He has an inconsistent temperament, for example, which he displays when he makes sure the girl who delivers him the message gets something to eat but then erupts furiously at his wife only a few moments later. Additionally, he can be overly proud, as when he is dismayed by the fact that there are only lower-class people in his carriage and makes a boastful, false statement about his familiarity with Johannesburg. Kumalo is embarking on an emotional exploration of his homeland, and by making him fallible rather than flawless, Paton ensures that we will be able to empathize with Kumalo's experience.

BOOK I: CHAPTERS 4–6

The white man has broken the tribe. . . . That is why children break the law, and old white people are robbed and beaten. (See QUOTATIONS, p. 65)

SUMMARY — CHAPTER 4

The train to Johannesburg travels a full day and night, climbing through many hills and villages. The regions Kumalo passes through are unfamiliar to him, with foreign landscapes and signs written in Afrikaans, which he does not speak. The great mines of South Africa come into view, and Kumalo's fellow travelers, many of whom are miners, explain how the mines are painstakingly excavated. They point out the great pulley that hoists the broken rocks, and Kumalo is awestruck by the scale of it all. Overwhelmed by the modern surroundings, he keeps mistaking the passing landscape for Johannesburg, but his fellow passengers laugh and tell him of buildings in Johannesburg so tall they can barely describe them.

The train arrives in Johannesburg, where Kumalo moves gingerly through the crowds that swarm throughout the station. Outside the station, the rush of traffic so terrifies Kumalo that he stands petrified on the sidewalk, unable to decipher the traffic lights. Speaking in a language Kumalo does not understand, a young man appears and offers to help Kumalo find his way to Sophiatown.

The young man leads Kumalo to the bus station, where he tells Kumalo to wait in line for the buses while the young man buys him a ticket. Eager to show his trust, Kumalo gives the young man a pound from his precious savings. He begins to suspect that something is wrong, however, as soon as the young man turns the corner. An elderly man takes pity on the helpless Kumalo and informs him that his money has been stolen. When it turns out that they are both headed for Sophiatown, the elderly man invites Kumalo to travel with him. He guides Kumalo safely to Msimangu's Mission House, where the young Reverend Msimangu opens the door and introduces Kumalo's companion as Mr. Mafolo. Mr. Mafolo takes his leave as Kumalo, safe at last, enjoys a cigarette and reflects on the days to come.

Summary — Chapter 5

Msimangu informs Kumalo that he has found a room for him with Mrs. Lithebe, a local churchgoer. Kumalo uses a modern toilet for the first time—in his village, he had heard of these devices, but he had never used one. The two men dine with the other priests, a group that includes both blacks and whites, at the mission. Kumalo speaks sadly and lovingly about his village, and about how both Ixopo and its neighboring villages are falling into ruin. One white rosy-cheeked priest wishes to hear more, but he excuses himself to attend to other affairs. The other priests, in turn, tell Kumalo that all is not well in Johannesburg—white people have become afraid because of a rise in crime. They show him a newspaper headline describing an attack on an elderly white couple. Nor are whites the only victims, they say, and they tell him how an African girl was robbed and almost raped.

After dinner, Msimangu asks Kumalo about Gertrude. Kumalo replies that his sister came to Johannesburg with her child to find her husband. Msimangu regretfully informs him that she now has many husbands—she sells cheap liquor and prostitutes herself in the worst area of Johannesburg. There have been crimes committed at her home, and she has been in prison. Msimangu also tells a distraught Kumalo that Gertrude's son lives with her, but that her home is no place for a child. Msimangu has heard nothing about

Absalom but promises to ask about him. As the sorrowful Kumalo goes to pray, he asks about his brother, and Msimangu informs him that John Kumalo is now a great politician but has little use for the church.

Msimangu explains that he does not hate the white man, in part because a white man "brought [his] father out of darkness" by converting him to Christianity. He confides to Kumalo, nevertheless, that he believes that white people have broken the tribal structure without leaving anything in its place. Msimangu explains that some white men are trying to rebuild the country for all people, but that they are not enough, and are held prisoner by the same fear that rules the rest of the country. He says that Father Vincent, the rosy-cheeked priest at dinner, is the best person to ask about such things. Kumalo retires to his lodgings and marvels that only forty-eight hours ago he had been with his wife.

SUMMARY — CHAPTER 6

Msimangu accompanies Kumalo to the neighboring slums of Claremont, where Gertrude lives. It is a pity, Msimangu says, that the neighborhoods are not farther apart—the trams are filled with rival gangs of hooligans, and there is always trouble. Despite their pretty names, the streets of Claremont are filthy, and Msimangu points out a woman who is a prominent liquor dealer and explains that many of the children in the streets are not at school because there is no room for them in the classes. Msimangu waits up the street while Kumalo listens to the strange, unfriendly laughter coming from behind his sister's door. Gertrude keeps Kumalo waiting while her unseen companions hastily rearrange and prepare the room.

Gertrude is sullen and fearful at first, and she tells Kumalo that she has not yet found her husband. Kumalo reproaches her for not writing and demands to see her child. When it becomes clear that she does not know where the child is, he tells Gertrude that she has shamed them, and announces that he has come to take her back. She falls on the ground in hysterics, saying that she wants to leave Johannesburg but is not a good enough person to return home. Softened by her remorse, Kumalo forgives her, and they pray together.

Although Gertrude and Kumalo are now reconciled, she is unable to give him news of his son, although she says that their nephew—John's son—has spent time with Absalom and that he will know. A neighborhood woman brings in Gertrude's son, and Kumalo urges his sister to collect her things while he secures her a room at Mrs. Lithebe's. Kumalo returns with a borrowed truck to collect Gertrude, and, in the evening, greatly encouraged by the success of this first mission, he feels as if the tribe is being rebuilt and the soul of his home restored.

ANALYSIS — BOOK I: CHAPTERS 4–6

Kumalo's inability to understand his surroundings throughout these chapters underscores that his visit to Johannesburg is a rite of passage for him. The novel leaps forward from Natal directly to the outskirts of Johannesburg, and the novel's omission of Kumalo's actual journey means that we see the abrupt change in landscapes without a smooth transition. From the train window, everything is immediately and overwhelmingly different: the dominant language is now Afrikaans (a Dutch-based language spoken by the original white immigrants to South Africa), and the black Africans are from different tribes. The shared points of reference that characterize village life are gone—when a man on the train likens the height of the buildings in Johannesburg to a hill behind his father's home, Kumalo does not know what he is talking about. Even familiar sights and sounds appear to be corrupted. Behind Gertrude's door, Kumalo hears the sound of laughter, but even this sound is so twisted that it is more terrifying than reassuring.

On the other hand, Kumalo is also quick to adapt. He finds the lavatory at Msimangu's Mission House a curiosity, but he is able to use it without difficulty. It is true that Kumalo requires Msimangu's help just to find Gertrude's place, but, impressively, he returns that same afternoon with a truck and is able to help his sister move. Initially unable to decipher even the smallest details of city life, such as a traffic light, Kumalo learns rapidly and shows remarkable resourcefulness despite his foreign surroundings.

Though intimidating, Johannesburg is not wholly symbolic of evil in the world. There are factors that ease Kumalo's transition and that more generally provide hope that all is not lost for South Africa. Kumalo is helped and treated with respect by the men he speaks to on the train and by Mr. Mafolo. It would seem, then, that the young man who robs Kumalo is an exception, not the rule. The priests at the mission sit together regardless of color, demonstrating that racial harmony is possible, and they greet Kumalo's story with friendship and interest. Thus, although Johannesburg, with its chaotic nature, has the potential to destroy individuals and families, as

Gertrude's separation from her child demonstrates, it also has the power to bring people together.

This section shows the complicated relationship between Christianity and white domination. On the one hand, the priests of the mission appear to be the only people both concerned enough and strong enough to heal the city's wounds. Furthermore, Msimangu appreciates that a white man "brought [his] father out of darkness" by converting him to Christianity, demonstrating that some natives welcome this religion imported from Europe. On the other hand, Christianity is partly responsible for the decimation of the tribal structure in South Africa. With two separate communities whose values differ so greatly—the indigenous South African tribes and the transplanted white colonists—so deeply ingrained in the cultural landscape of South Africa, it seems unlikely that one would wholly suppress the other. Kumalo is caught between these two communities, as evidenced by the fact that he often refers to God as "*Tixo*," the Xosa word for "Great Spirit," instead of using European words. This apparent synthesis of his Zulu and Christian heritages suggests that Kumalo has managed to find a middle ground between these cultures.

BOOK I: CHAPTERS 7–9

> *I see only one hope for our country, and that is when white men and black men . . . desiring only the good of their country, come together to work for it. . . .*
> (See QUOTATIONS, p. 66)

SUMMARY — CHAPTER 7

Kumalo sits in his lodgings, writing a letter to his wife and listening to Gertrude sing as she helps Mrs. Lithebe around the house while her son plays in the garden. Msimangu arrives and brings Kumalo to the shop of his brother, John. Although John does not recognize Kumalo at first, he seems pleasantly surprised to see him. Kumalo learns that John's wife, Esther, has left him, and that John has since acquired a mistress.

John tries to explain why he stopped writing home and then asks Kumalo if he may speak in English. In a strange voice, he relates that he has been seized by "an experience" in Johannesburg that has made him see things differently. In the village, John says, he was a nobody and had to obey the chief, whom he calls ignorant and a tool of the white man. In Johannesburg, he says, he is free from the chief, although he adds that the church serves a similar function in keeping black South Africans down. Things are changing in Johannesburg, John proclaims, and his voice deepens with emotion as he decries the wealth and power of the mine's owners and the poverty of the miners. Although the bishop condemns this economic discrepancy, he lives in a fancy house, which embitters John toward the church.

Msimangu questions John's fidelity to his former wife. Before John can respond, Kumalo intervenes and John's mistress silently serves tea. Kumalo confesses that listening to John is painful for him, both because of John's manner of speaking and because much of what he says is true. He tells John he has found Gertrude and asks about Absalom. John says he does not know where either Absalom or his own son are, then remembers that they were working in a textile factory in Alexandra. Msimangu and Kumalo take their leave.

As they head to the textile factory, Msimangu explains to Kumalo that much of what John said is true, and that John is one of the three most important black men in Johannesburg. Msimangu also suggests, however, that if John were as courageous as he maintains, he would be in prison, and Msimangu observes that power can corrupt even the most dedicated politician.

At the textile factory, the white men who manage the plant are helpful, stating that Absalom has not worked there for twelve months. Kumalo and Msimangu meet a friend of Absalom's who says that Absalom used to live with a Mrs. Ndlela in Sophiatown. The two priests find Mrs. Ndlela, who tells them that Absalom has moved to Alexandra. After Kumalo steps outside, Msimangu asks Mrs. Ndlela why she seems so sorry for Kumalo, and she reveals that both she and her husband felt that Absalom kept bad company.

SUMMARY — CHAPTER 8

Msimangu and Kumalo catch a bus to Alexandra from Johannesburg. As they board the bus, however, they are stopped by Dubula, another of the three most important black leaders in Johannesburg. Dubula tells them that blacks are boycotting the buses because the fares have been raised and persuades them to walk the eleven miles to Alexandra. As they walk, they accept a ride from a white driver, who goes miles out of his way to help them.

Kumalo and Msimangu walk the remaining distance as Msimangu explains that in Alexandra, blacks are allowed to own property, but that the town is so crime-ridden that its white neighbors have petitioned to have it destroyed. He tells Kumalo stories of whites being attacked and killed, and ends with the moving story of a black couple's rescue of a white woman who had been raped and abandoned by a white man. He also says, however, that Alexandra is more good than bad.

Kumalo and Msimangu reach Absalom's new house, but its owner, Mrs. Mkize, is visibly afraid and will tell them only that Absalom moved a year ago. Kumalo knows that something is wrong, and Msimangu tells him to go on ahead and seek refreshment, then returns to question the woman again. She is too scared to say what she knows, but when Msimangu swears on a Bible to keep her secret safe, she reveals that Absalom and John's son often came home very late at night with all kinds of money, food, watches, and clothes.

Mrs. Mkize tells him that both boys were friends with a local taxi driver named Hlabeni. Msimangu hires Hlabeni to drive him and Kumalo back to Johannesburg, then asks Hlabeni if he knows Absalom's whereabouts. Hlabeni, who is scared, admits that the young men now live in a shantytown in the city of Orlando. They drive past crowds of black people resolutely walking instead of taking the bus, while a number of white drivers offer them rides. Msimangu is particularly impressed by the behavior of one white driver who has been pulled over by the police, and he slaps his chest and defiantly echoes the driver's cry of "take me to court."

SUMMARY — CHAPTER 9

A chorus of anonymous voices describes Shanty Town. From all over the land, people pour into the city of Johannesburg. The waiting lists for houses are impossibly long, however, and there is little room in the houses in Alexandra, Sophiatown, and Orlando. Families with homes take in boarders, but the accommodations fill up, often with a dozen people crammed into two rooms. Privacy is scarce, and tempers flare. Some husbands and wives are seduced by their lodgers; others throw tenants out into the street in fits of protective jealousy. A well-placed bribe may secure the right person a home, but there are no guarantees. The money to build housing is tied up because of war in Europe and North Africa.

Dubula's commands ripple through the masses of the homeless. Building supplies are stolen from the plantations, train stations, and mines. Near Orlando's railroad tracks, an entire city goes up overnight, made of poles, sacks, and the long grasses of the South African plains. The only cost is a shilling a week to Dubula's committee. It is crowded and wet in Shanty Town. In the middle of the night, a child burns with fever and dies before a doctor can reach her. Newspapermen come and take pictures, and the state springs into action. New homes are built for the Shanty Town masses, just as Dubula said they would be.

But a new tide of people rushes to set up makeshift homes, and this time the state reacts with anger. The police drive these people back to where they came from. A few remain, watching the new houses that the government is building and waiting for their turn to move in.

ANALYSIS — BOOK I: CHAPTERS 7–9

By introducing the figure of John Kumalo, these chapters give us a political context for Stephen Kumalo's journey. John's claim that the local village chiefs are pawns of the white man is somewhat accurate—historically, white leaders in South Africa allowed tribal chiefs free rein as long as the chiefs did not interfere with white claims to power. Similarly, John's claims that the church preaches submission and meekness, that the old village way of life is dying, and that a new way of life is being born in Johannesburg are also true. Msimangu's earlier comment about his father being carried out of the "darkness" into Christianity reflects that he has submitted himself to a new order. Furthermore, it is clear that Johannesburg, with its prostitution and liquor-selling, represents a corruption of old village values.

Despite his insightful viewpoints, however, John is an unreliable representative of these old village values. He has broken his family ties by parting with his wife, probably due to his infidelity, and by ceasing to correspond with his family. He is more comfortable speaking in English than in his native Zulu, and he addresses his brother as if he were making a speech to an invisible audience. Furthermore, he seems overly impressed, rather than disgusted, by European prosperity. Finally, Msimangu hints that John does not have the courage to match his convictions—John fears taking real risks to improve the lot of black Africans. John speaks out against white oppression, but he does so more from personal egotism than out of genuine concern for his people. Although he is correct in many ways, John possesses many of the flaws of the system he criticizes.

Msimangu, on the other hand, stands for the incorruptible power of love, and these chapters validate his claim that there is "only one hope for our country . . . when white men and black men . . . desiring only the good of their country, come together to work for it." The story of the black couple who helps a destitute white woman, for example, shows that racial harmony and human decency are possible, even if the government seems unable or unwilling to operate in accordance with these ideals. While John operates from corrupt motivations, his friend and colleague Dubula, who seems to work tirelessly and selflessly for his people, leads the bus boycott to protest economic prejudice against blacks. Solidarity between whites and blacks triumphs over racism as white South Africans risk trouble with the police in order to give rides to the striking blacks, and Msimangu, impressed with this display, takes up and repeats one white man's defiant challenge to the police, "Take me to court."

In an overview of black Shanty Town life in Chapter 9, Paton employs an unusual narrative technique of setting aside the novel's story line and meditates on South Africa's physical and social landscape. Paton uses this same technique in Chapters 1, 3, and 4 in describing the geography of South Africa. In Chapter 9, however, the description is focused more on the country's social landscape. Repetitive scraps of dialogue from anonymous speakers are woven together, giving a sense of the general desperation of these settlements. We hear the voices of need as one clambering, undifferentiated mass: the voices of those who need lodging and the voices of those who need money and who are thus forced to rent out precious space. Finally, the action focuses on one woman and her sick daughter, for whom a doctor is found only after it is too late. The destruction of this small family mirrors the greater destruction of African life as a whole.

BOOK I: CHAPTERS 10–12

*Cry for the broken tribe, for the law and the custom
that is gone. Aye, and cry aloud for the man who is
dead, for the woman and children bereaved. Cry, the
beloved country. . . .* (See QUOTATIONS, p. 67)

SUMMARY — CHAPTER 10

While waiting to go to Shanty Town, Kumalo spends time with Gertrude and her son. He and Gertrude have little to say to each other, but he takes comfort in telling his small nephew about Natal, and Gertrude finds a friend in Mrs. Lithebe. In Shanty Town, Kumalo and Msimangu ask a nurse about Absalom's whereabouts. The nurse sends them to Mrs. Hlatshwayo, with whom Absalom was staying. She tells them that Absalom was sent to the reformatory. As they walk to the reformatory, Msimangu tries to comfort Kumalo, saying that he has heard good things about the reformatory. To Msimangu's surprise, Kumalo asks him what he spoke about with Mrs. Mkize, Absalom's landlady in Alexandra. Msimangu reveals that she told him that Absalom and John's son often came home late with bundles of white people's possessions.

At the reformatory, a young white man tells Msimangu and Kumalo that Absalom was a model student, but that he was discharged a month earlier because of his age, good behavior, and the frequent visits from his pregnant girlfriend. Despite Kumalo's worry that the young man will be unsympathetic to a black man who speaks no Afrikaans, the young man is quite helpful. He promises to take Msimangu and Kumalo to Absalom's new home in Pimville, where, the young man says, Absalom is saving money and preparing to marry his girlfriend.

The young man, Msimangu, and Kumalo go to Absalom's house in Pimville, where Absalom's girlfriend, still a child herself, tells them that Absalom left the house a few days earlier and has not yet returned. Kumalo asks her what she will do, but before she can respond, Msimangu speaks harshly to the girl and tells Kumalo that her problem is one that Kumalo cannot solve. When Kumalo protests that she carries his grandchild, Msimangu scoffs at the idea and wonders out loud how many other children Absalom may have. After informing them that Absalom has been absent from work for many days, the young man leaves them at the gates of Orlando, where Msimangu apologizes to Kumalo for his unkind words. Kumalo forgives him and asks Msimangu to take him back to the girl.

SUMMARY — CHAPTER 11

Msimangu persuades Kumalo to take a few days' rest while Msimangu goes to Ezenzeleni, a colony for the blind. Kumalo and Msimangu then enjoy a quiet evening at the Mission House with Father Vincent, who listens to Kumalo's stories of Natal and tells them about his native England. The tranquil evening is shattered, however, when another priest enters with a newspaper whose front page announces the murder of Arthur Jarvis, a white engineer and crusader for the rights of black South Africans. Jarvis, the paper reports, was at home with a cold when intruders knocked out his servant and shot him at close range. The paper states that there are no leads, but police hope the unconscious servant will be able to furnish some information upon awakening. The paper also states that Jarvis was in the midst of writing his treatise on "The Truth About Native Crime" when he was murdered. The article closes by saying that Jarvis leaves behind a widow and two children—a nine-year-old son and a five-year-old daughter.

Kumalo remembers seeing Arthur as a boy, small and bright, with his father—the Jarvis farm overlooks Ndotsheni. He is weighed down by a sudden, inexplicable fear. Msimangu tries to reassure him that the odds of any connection between Absalom and the murder are small, but Kumalo is inconsolable and too tired even to pray.

SUMMARY — CHAPTER 12

A speaker notes that no one can enjoy the beauty of South Africa amid so much violence. The speaker adds that throughout the nation, thousands of voices cry out what must be done. This speaker argues that there should be more police, and another speaker argues that if black Africans had more rights, there would be less crime. Some advocate that more schools be built in the black districts, where fewer than half the children go to school, but others say that schooling blacks only produces criminals who are more clever. The pass laws that require native South Africans to carry permits in white areas might work, says one man, but his friend counters that these laws can't be enforced and imprison innocent people. Some argue for greater segregation, others for greater education and opportunities. Disagreement is the only certainty, and the white population lives barricaded behind their fear.

Mrs. Ndlela, whom Msimangu and Kumalo visited earlier in their search for Absalom, tells Msimangu that the police have visited her looking for Absalom and that she referred them to Mrs. Mkize. Before Msimangu can slip out on his own to investigate, however, he runs into Kumalo. He allows Kumalo to come along. The two retrace their search, going first to Mrs. Mkize, then to Shanty Town, and then to the reformatory school, where the young man's assistant tells them that the young man seems troubled. Their last stop is Alexandra, where Absalom's girlfriend tells them that the police have visited her but that she does not know why, and a local woman says that the police seemed frustrated. Everyone agrees that the situation looks serious. Kumalo spends more of his precious savings on a taxi, and the two men begin a somber trip to Ezenzeleni.

Analysis — Book I: Chapters 10–12

This section opens with a lyrical meditation on hope and ends with a lyrical litany of despair. At the outset, Kumalo takes strength from his nephew, a serious but affectionate youngster who seems to reconnect Kumalo to his village life. The act of telling the child about his village eases Kumalo's homesickness and, though he is saddened by the thought of his son, strengthens Kumalo with thoughts of his wife and friends in the village. Kumalo's interaction with his nephew thus reaffirms Kumalo's values. But Kumalo faces a gradually worsening picture of Absalom's situation, and Paton builds our sense of foreboding to match Kumalo's. The details of Absalom's situation are teased out as we discover, piece by piece, that he has been in trouble with the law, has impregnated a young girl, and has now disappeared. Each stop on Msimangu and Kumalo's zigzagging journey brings a new clue. The announcement of Jarvis's murder seems, at first, to be merely a part of the social landscape. Paton, however, makes it a climactic moment in Kumalo's quest for knowledge about Absalom, introducing it at just the right point to make us suspect that Absalom is involved with the murder. The narrative structure skillfully leads us to have the same suspicions that Kumalo has.

Arthur Jarvis's murder demonstrates the terrible ironies of the social disorder that mars the country. Jarvis wishes to help black Africans regain their rights. Presumably, his tract on native crime explains that the solution to the problem lies in greater freedom and opportunity for the black population, not in greater suppression. The tragic irony, then, is the fact that he is murdered by people for whose rights he is fighting. We can assume that his killers are motivated at least in part by the desperation created by the inequities of South African society. Although Jarvis fights these inequities, his attackers perceive him not as an ally but as part of the problem since he is white.

By juxtaposing a number of different white voices in Chapter 12, some of which are sympathetic and some that are profoundly unsympathetic to the black Africans, Paton lays bare the stark differences of opinion that divide the white population. The man who bemoans the lack of adequate education for black children in Johannesburg represents the belief that the white government is responsible for the natives' problems because it has failed to help empower blacks. The man who worries that more schooling will make blacks smarter criminals, on the other hand, represents the belief that the black population is inherently immoral. Whereas the first man embodies trust in the black population, the second man embodies mistrust of the black population. Those who fall on the side of the second speaker seem oblivious to the challenges facing the black population, and Paton suggests that these whites remain oblivious on purpose because of their fear.

BOOK I: CHAPTERS 13–15

SUMMARY — CHAPTER 13

Kumalo and Msimangu travel to Ezenzeleni, a colony where white South Africans care for blind black South Africans. Msimangu has work to do here, so Kumalo sits by himself for some time and meditates. The thoughts of his grandson being born out of wedlock, his son's thievery, and the murder bring him to despair, but he takes heart at the thought of returning to Ndotsheni with new humility. Kumalo's newfound high spirits evaporate as he admits to himself that the ways of the tribe have been lost forever. When Msimangu returns and finds Kumalo in despair, Msimangu reminds Kumalo that despair is a sin.

Kumalo is comforted by the help given to the blind in Ezenzeleni and especially by Msimangu's rousing sermon to the blind. He knows that Msimangu speaks to him when he says God will not forsake humankind. Some people criticize Msimangu for using his preaching gifts to teach patience while so many of his people die, but Kumalo feels spiritually refreshed.

SUMMARY — CHAPTER 14

Gertrude's furniture, the final remnants of her past, are sold at a great profit, but Kumalo feels only fear when he sees Msimangu approach Mrs. Lithebe's house with the young man from the reformatory. The man tells him that his fears have been justified, that Absalom is in jail for the murder of Arthur Jarvis and that Absalom fired the shot. John's son was with Absalom during the crime, and Kumalo goes to break the news to his brother. Devastated by the news, John goes with Kumalo to the mission, where Father Vincent offers them help, and the young man from the reformatory leads them to the prison.

In the prison's visiting room, Kumalo and Absalom are finally reunited, but Absalom cannot look his father in the eye. He shifts and squirms and blames his condition on bad company and the devil, to Kumalo's disgust, and tears up when the young man reproaches him for rejecting the lessons of the reformatory. Absalom states that he shot Jarvis, but he explains that he fired only because he was afraid, and maintains that he still wants to marry his girlfriend.

At the prison gates, Kumalo meets John again, but John is no longer in despair. He will get his son a lawyer, he says, adding that there is no proof that his son was even present at the time of the murder. Kumalo, John cruelly states, will not need a lawyer—his son is guilty and cannot be saved. The young man, embittered by his disappointment with Absalom, refuses to advise Kumalo and defiantly asserts that his work at the reformatory is important. He drives off, John leaves on foot, and Kumalo is left alone. Father Vincent, he decides, is his only hope.

SUMMARY — CHAPTER 15

Before Kumalo can seek out Father Vincent, the man from the reformatory returns to apologize for his harsh language. He advises Kumalo that he will need a lawyer because John is untrustworthy. He says they need someone who will make sure John's claim that his son was not there does not hurt Absalom, and who will argue that Absalom fired because he was afraid.

Kumalo and the young man go to see Father Vincent, and he tells them that he has a lawyer in mind and that he will also help with Absalom's marriage. The young man leaves, and Kumalo speaks about his grief to Father Vincent. He is especially upset that he and his wife had no idea what was happening to their son in Johannesburg and that he has only found out now that it is too late. He is also wounded by his son's apparent lack of remorse. Father Vincent is pained by Kumalo's statements, but he reminds Kumalo that at least his sorrow has replaced his fear and that his son may well still be able to repent for his great evil. Kumalo allows himself a rare moment of bitterness, but Father Vincent refuses to let him remain cynical, insisting that Kumalo keep up the rituals of his religion in order to make true faith return.

ANALYSIS — BOOK I: CHAPTERS 13–15

In these chapters, which form the climax of the novel, the Kumalo family becomes a model for coping with great suffering, and Paton uses Kumalo's experiences to show how grief can prompt a range of emotional responses. At times, we see Kumalo so smitten by sorrow that he is unable to function and simply shuts down. Kumalo, rendered completely mute and unable to do anything but nod, temporarily comes to a complete halt when he first hears the news about his son, and he seems to have great difficulty holding on to his sanity. Absalom is similarly unable to function. Pressed for answers in the prison's visiting room, he mostly nods, cries, or says he doesn't know. In these instances, Kumalo and his son epitomize grief as a kind of paralysis, during which even the everyday functions of the body, like talking or moving, are impossible.

On the other hand, the novel suggests various ways that individuals can derive meaning from sorrow and find solace in it. Christianity plays an important role in this process. Both Msimangu and Father Vincent comfort Kumalo with words from the Bible. Father Vincent reminds him that the ways of God are secret and suggests to him that he must find meaning by showing his compassion for others, rather than by trying to understand why Absalom has gone astray. The ability to accept the idea that there is a divine plan for the universe leads to a sense of order that provides refuge when everyday life seems disorderly or cruel. Comforting others provides a similar refuge. Kumalo has always gotten strength from helping others, as evidenced by his rejuvenation when he finds and rescues Gertrude. In Chapter 15, Father Vincent confirms the idea that helping others can bring relief to one's own soul. Kumalo's suffering is so unbearable for Father Vincent to see that he wonders when the old man's painful ruminations will cease, looks away, and can barely sit still. Father Vincent also has his moment of paralysis while the two men sit together in silence, but he recovers his sense of well-being by reminding Kumalo of God's mercy and helping him keep his faith and find solace.

Throughout these three chapters, Kumalo is frequently left alone, and the scenes paint a somewhat negative portrait of solitude. In Ezenzeleni's garden, Kumalo is unable to remain hopeful, even at the prospect of returning with his newfound knowledge of ways to heal Ndotsheni. In the mission, he rejects Father Vincent's suggestion that he pray, dismissing it so bitterly that Father Vincent is forced to sit the old parson down for a priestly intervention. Most poignant of all is Kumalo's abandonment at the prison gates. The scene is set with great drama, with the young man driving off angrily in one direction and John setting off in another, leaving Kumalo conspicuously alone.

BOOK I: CHAPTERS 16–17

SUMMARY — CHAPTER 16

Kumalo, who has begun to find his way around Johannesburg, goes to Pimville on his own to visit Absalom's girlfriend. She has not heard the news about Absalom, and when Kumalo tells her, she is devastated. Kumalo asks Absalom's girlfriend if she still wishes to marry Absalom, and though she says she does, she seems confused. Kumalo presses her further, and she explains that her father left her mother because her mother was always drunk. She disliked her mother's new boyfriend, so she ran away from home. Even though Absalom's girlfriend is still almost a child herself, she has had three lovers since she left home. Her lovers, whom she calls "husbands," have all been arrested. Kumalo is angered by her promiscuity and harshly asks her if she would accept him as a lover. Frightened and confused, she says she would.

Shocked by her answer, Kumalo covers his face with his hands, and she begins crying and lamenting. Ashamed of his behavior, Kumalo comforts her and asks if she would like to come with him to Ndotsheni and live with his family as their daughter. She gratefully responds that she would and assures him that her only desire is a quiet life. Kumalo is surprised to find himself laughing with pleasure, and after making Absalom's girlfriend promise to tell him if she ever regrets her decision, he goes off to find her a new place to stay.

SUMMARY — CHAPTER 17

Although Gertrude and Mrs. Lithebe get along, Mrs. Lithebe worries that Gertrude has a strange carelessness about her and is too friendly with strange men. Still, Mrs. Lithebe admires and respects Kumalo, and she agrees to let Absalom's girlfriend move in. Kumalo, ecstatic with Mrs. Lithebe's reply, plays with his nephew. Absalom's girlfriend moves in and behaves with appropriate modesty. One day, however, Mrs. Lithebe comes upon Gertrude and Absalom's girlfriend laughing in a way she does not like. She calls Absalom's girlfriend to her and tells her that she must not laugh in this way, and the girl immediately understands and agrees. Gertrude continues with her strange behavior, though she now leaves Absalom's girlfriend alone.

Kumalo goes to visit Absalom, who tells him that Absalom's friends are denying that they were in the house with Absalom. Absalom gradually comes to agree with his father that his companions are not true friends. Absalom is pleased, however, by the prospect of having a lawyer, and he promises Kumalo that he will tell the lawyer nothing but the truth. He is also happy with the arrangements Kumalo has made for Absalom's girlfriend. On his way out, Kumalo passes Absalom's lawyer, a dignified white man with the air of a "chief."

Some time later, the lawyer, Mr. Carmichael, visits Kumalo at the mission house. Absalom's defense will be based on the truth, he says, and he will need as much information about Absalom's character as possible. After Mr. Carmichael leaves, Kumalo frets about the legal costs, but Father Vincent informs him that Mr. Carmichael will take the case *pro deo*, or "for God"—meaning he will take case for free.

ANALYSIS — BOOK I: CHAPTERS 16–17

Though their lives somewhat resemble each other's, Absalom's girlfriend and Gertrude represent two distinct models of womanhood in the novel. Whereas Gertrude, enmeshed in her seedy Johannesburg life of prostitution and liquor-selling, is cynical, Absalom's girlfriend, who is young and unwise to the ways of the world, is optimistic. This difference in attitude is reflected in their different reactions to Kumalo's invitation to return with him to Ndotsheni. Gertrude initially turns down Kumalo's invitation because she considers herself too sinful. But Absalom's girlfriend, who, like Gertrude, is promiscuous, immediately accepts Kumalo's offer because she attributes much of her misfortune to the circumstances of her past and not to her own actions. Gertrude sees no hope for her situation, while Absalom's girlfriend has complete faith, perhaps naïvely, that blessings such as marriage and family can rehabilitate her.

Both Kumalo and Msimangu reproach Absalom's girlfriend for her lifestyle, but she in fact shares many of Kumalo's values, including an emphasis on family. She runs away from her own family, but she does so not because she dislikes the mutual dependency involved with belonging to a family—having to depend on others and having others depend on her. Rather, she leaves home because her deteriorating family fails to offer nurturing relationships. She fulfills her need for such relationships by taking lovers, whom she calls "husbands," a term that demonstrates her desire to interact with others on a meaningful level. Similarly, her unreserved willingness to give herself to Kumalo—as either a lover or a daughter (she is quick to call Kumalo her new "father")—illustrates how desperate she is to be loved. Stripped of everything by her circumstances, Absalom's girlfriend still craves the family structure that Kumalo considers so important, and she makes do with what pieces of it she can find.

Gertrude's strange behavior marks a fundamental perversity in her character, and it signals the novel's tendency to relegate native women to the domestic sphere. The arrival of Absalom's girlfriend makes it clear that black South African women endure a second type of segregation by being confined to their homes. Although it is mentioned that women are seen on the streets, every female character that the novel portrays as respectable speaks from inside her home: Mrs. Mkize, Mrs. Ndlela, and Mrs. Lithebe. Clearly, there is little value in the violence and degradation of Gertrude's old life, but it is not surprising that she chafes at the strict rules that govern her life at Mrs. Lithebe's house. The novel, however, presents Gertrude's resistance to strictly defined gender roles as if it were a sign of mental illness. The novel deals too often with forgiveness to condemn Gertrude's actions explicitly, but the fact that nobody can quite describe her strange laughter and carelessness makes her seem deranged. What one might reasonably see as resistance to domestication is instead shown as borderline insanity.

Mr. Carmichael carries himself like a "chief," a description that gives some credit to the cultural institutions of native South Africans. In earlier chapters, John Kumalo calls the chiefs ignorant, and he likens them to the white man's dogs. Mr. Carmichael, however, is a man of dignity and respect, and, even though he is white, he is a great friend and leader of black South Africans. He is a man of integrity who exists above the dominant prejudice of his era. Since he is the novel's first example of a chief, his position seems like it is one of great responsibility and wisdom, one of the offices in South Africa capable of crossing racial lines. This impression of Mr. Carmichael is only fleeting and the position of chief becomes much less glamorous in later chapters, but the figure of Mr. Carmichael demonstrates what the chief once was and suggests what the chief has the potential to become.

BOOK II: CHAPTERS 18–21

The truth is that our civilization is not Christian; it is a tragic compound of great ideal and fearful practice. . . . (See QUOTATIONS, p. 68)

SUMMARY — CHAPTER 18

The narrator repeats the descriptions of the hills of Natal that open Book I: the valleys are lovely, and the grass is thick and green. Looking down upon it all is High Place, the residence of a white farmer named James Jarvis, the father of the slain Arthur Jarvis. Jarvis hopes that rain will soon fall on his dry fields. The hills of Ndotsheni below are dry and barren from over-farming, and no one knows how to solve the problem. Jarvis ponders all the possible solutions to the over-farming. If only the native people would learn how to farm, he thinks, and if only those who were educated stayed to help their people instead of running to the city. Of course, his own son, Arthur, decided to leave the farm and become an engineer in Johannesburg, but he doesn't begrudge Arthur his decision.

Standing on a ridge to look for rain clouds, Jarvis sees a police car approaching his home. He thinks that it must be one of the Afrikaner policemen—Afrikaners are white South Africans of Dutch descent largely considered by families of English descent to be of a lower class. Though he is of English descent, Jarvis believes that the local Afrikaners are a fine people. Two policemen, van Jaarsveld and Binnendyk, come to him with the shocking news that his son has been shot and killed. As Jarvis copes with the announcement, they offer to make arrangements to get him to Johannesburg as quickly as possible. He accepts their offer, and while one of the policemen calls to arrange for the flight, Jarvis breaks the bad news to his wife, who breaks down crying and screaming.

SUMMARY — CHAPTER 19

Mr. Jarvis and his wife fly to Johannesburg and are greeted by John Harrison, the brother of their son's wife, Mary. They travel to the house of John and Mary's parents, where they meet Mary, her mother, and her father, Mr. Harrison. Jarvis, his wife, and Mary get into the car with John to go the mortuary. On the way there, John tells Jarvis that Arthur was an advocate for the rights of the country's natives, an issue on which Mr. Harrison and Arthur did not see eye-to-eye.

After seeing Arthur's body, the family returns to the Harrisons', where Jarvis joins Mr. Harrison for a drink. Mr. Harrison tells him that condolence messages have poured in from every part of the community, including from the prime minister and mayor. He tells Jarvis that Arthur could speak Afrikaans and Zulu, that he was interested in learning Sesuto (a native language like Zulu), and that some wanted him to run for parliament. Arthur protested the housing conditions of the mines' workers, ignoring warnings that he was jeopardizing his job as an engineer and maintaining that the truth was more important than money. Mr. Harrison calls Arthur a real crusader in his efforts for others, then reveals that all of white Johannesburg is scared stiff by the attacks. Though neither he nor Mr. Harrison share Arthur's politics, Jarvis is moved by these stories about the respect his son inspired and about his son's courage.

Jarvis goes to bed, where he shares the stories with his wife and expresses his regret that he did not know more about his son while Arthur was alive. He falls asleep in his wife's arms, tormented by the question of why his son was murdered.

SUMMARY — CHAPTER 20

Jarvis sits in his son's house and looks at all his son's books and papers. He notices that his son seems to have particularly admired Abraham Lincoln. Jarvis finds a letter addressed to Arthur from a boys' club in the town of Claremont. He finds part of an article that his son was writing. In this article, Arthur argues that it is unacceptable to keep black South Africans unskilled in order to provide labor for the mines, to break up African family life by housing only black workers but not their families, to deny black Africans educational opportunities, and to break the tribal system without creating a new moral order in its place. Absorbed in his son's ideas and interested in learning more, Jarvis takes a copy of Lincoln's Gettysburg address. He then walks into the hallway where his son was killed and out of the house.

SUMMARY — CHAPTER 21

Arthur's funeral is packed with people from every walk of life, and for the first time, Jarvis sits in church with black people and shakes their hands. Afterward, Jarvis sits with Mr. Harrison. Mr. Harrison looks forward to getting revenge on Arthur's murderer, but Jarvis says that it is too early for him to think in these terms. Mr. Harrison speaks again about South Africa's problems: the natives are committing crimes and forming unions to demand higher wages and, in general, starting trouble. John joins them, and Mr. Harrison gets even more agitated, arguing against the white Afrikaners as well as black South Africans for claiming that the mines steal the country's natural resources. After asking John to take him to the boys' club some time, Jarvis retires to bed.

The next morning, Mr. Harrison tells Jarvis that he has received word that Arthur's servant has regained consciousness and has identified his assailant as a former garden boy of the Jarvises. He adds that the investigation can now move forward. Mr. Harrison also brings Jarvis the manuscript that Arthur was working on when he was killed. In this manuscript, Arthur argues that those who say God created black people to be unskilled laborers are un-Christian because they wish to prevent a segment of the population from developing their God-given abilities. The European rule of South Africa, Arthur's treatise says, is not a Christian one. Jarvis is deeply moved. He and his wife grieve that Arthur's life was cut off before he could finish his writing and his life's work.

ANALYSIS — BOOK II: CHAPTERS 18–21

In the beginning of Book II, we see South Africa from the perspective of a conservative white Englishman. The reasons for the impoverishment of the land in Ndotsheni are made explicit: black people are given a limited area to cultivate and over-farming of the land is the inevitable result. Furthermore, a lack of education and the flight of young people to cities make it difficult to introduce methods of farming that are more gentle to the land. The reasons for the ravaging of the land that Paton describes in the first three chapters are suddenly clear. The first two paragraphs of Book II are nearly identical to the first two paragraphs of Book I, which may suggest either the unlikelihood that these conditions will ever change or the inability of most white South Africans to understand the need for change.

The conservative and liberal sides of South Africa's pressing race debate find charming advocates in Mr. Harrison and in Arthur Jarvis. It is undeniable that Mr. Harrison's views of black Africans are severe, but he himself is a charming and sympathetic man. He brings comfort to the grief-stricken Jarvises, and although he acknowledges Arthur as a political opponent, he gives the dead man the appropriate amount of respect. Furthermore, his eloquent speech on how Johannesburg's white community lives in utter fear makes it clear that he is a captive of his emotions. Arthur, on the other hand, could be labeled an idealistic dreamer, but every glimpse we get of him is of a young man standing on a solid foundation of intelligence and moral strength. By providing such admirable champions of two white perspectives on race issues in South Africa, Paton forces us to focus on the issues themselves instead of allowing personalities to obscure them.

By examining Arthur Jarvis's ideas at length in this section, the novel provides a way for us to get an understanding of the views of those fighting against injustice in South Africa. In the two essay fragments that the novel includes, Arthur contrasts whites' justification of their policies to the policies' actual effects. In the first essay, Arthur lists what he thinks are the permissible assumptions and actions of whites: it is permissible to develop natural resources; it is permissible to recruit labor to work the mines; it is even permissible to permit the destruction of tribal life, which some believe was dying out anyway. Arthur argues, however, that it is not permissible to force black Africans to remain uneducated and unskilled just because the mines require unskilled labor. It is not permissible to house black workers but not their families now that the government understands that this set-up destroys family life. More generally, it is not permissible to develop natural resources at the cost of a group of people. Arthur's contention that "[s]uch development has only one true name, and that is exploitation" reflects his fundamental belief that blacks, as human beings, should receive the same treatment and be accorded the same dignity as whites.

Arthur's unfinished manuscript, which Mr. Harrison gives James Jarvis to read, validates the use of religion as a weapon against oppression. Until this point, Christianity has helped black South Africans endure the oppression of the country, but it has not helped them *resist* it. Arthur uses religion to argue against the policies of the mines. Contradicting the argument of white Christians that blacks were made to labor for whites, Arthur states bluntly that these men are falsely attributing their own opinions to God. A truly Christian leadership, Arthur argues, would encourage the cultivation of individual talents and skills among the native population. This argument provides a response to John Kumalo's earlier assertion that the church only reinforces white rule. Although the church can act as a voice for conservative, even oppressive ideas, the Christianity that Arthur Jarvis believes in stands on the side of black rights and demands change to the system that denies these rights.

BOOK II: CHAPTERS 22–24

SUMMARY — CHAPTER 22

Absalom's trial begins. Europeans sit on one side of the courtroom and non-Europeans sit on the other. The narrator notes that in South Africa, the judges are treated with great respect by all races, but though they are just, they often enforce unjust laws created by the white people. Absalom's two accomplices plead not guilty, but Absalom's lawyer says that Absalom will plead guilty only to "culpable homicide" since Absalom did not intend to kill Arthur Jarvis. The prosecutor denies this petition, however, and Absalom is forced to enter a plea of not guilty.

The other two defendants—John's son, Matthew, and a man named Johannes Pafuri—look sad and shocked while Absalom tells his side of the story. Absalom says that Johannes planned the robbery after hearing "a voice" that told him a time and date. After entering Arthur Jarvis's house, Absalom says, Johannes confronted Arthur's servant and demanded money and clothes. When the servant called out for his master, Johannes hit him over the head with an iron bar. Arthur burst in on the robbers, and Absalom fired his gun because he was frightened. He and his companions ran away. The judge asks Absalom why he brought the revolver, and Absalom says it was for his own protection. He also tells the court that Johannes brought the iron bar and claimed it had been blessed. The judge interrupts to ask Absalom if his father would bless such a weapon.

Absalom then resumes his narration: after the murder, he went to Mrs. Mkize's house, where he met his accomplices, then buried his revolver in a plantation field. He says that anyone—Mrs. Mkize, Matthew, or Johannes—who denies this claim is lying. He then says that he prayed for forgiveness. He spent the following day wandering around Johannesburg and ended up in a friend's house in Germiston. When the police found him there, they questioned him about Johannes, but Absalom told them that he himself shot Jarvis and indicated where the gun might be found. He meant to confess earlier, but he waited too long, and when the police arrived, he realized that waiting was a mistake. The court adjourns, and outside Kumalo sees Jarvis. He says nothing, however, because he feels that there is nothing he can possibly say to him.

Summary — Chapter 23

The trial receives little publicity because the front pages all carry news that gold has been discovered at Odendaalsrust. There is excitement at the stock exchange and talk of a "second Johannesburg" being built. Before the discovery of gold, the land was wasted, but the engineers' patience has finally paid off, and the stock prices are soaring. The English say that it is a shame that these prodigious feats of engineering should have such ugly Afrikaans names and that it is a shame that the Afrikaners cannot see that a bilingual state is a waste of time. In the spirit of unity, however, they keep their thoughts to themselves.

An anonymous conservative voice takes over the chapter, noting that some do-gooders want the new profits to go toward subsidizing social services or higher wages for the miners. This voice notes that it is a pity that these people, most of whom have no financial standing to speak of, are so good with words, such as a strange priest named Father Beresford. The thinking of these people is muddled, the voice says, and the narrator unjustly accuses the people of Johannesburg of being greedy when many of the town's prominent citizens actually give money to charities and collect art.

Another voice begins, this time one that is more liberal. It praises the work of Sir Ernest Oppenheimer, who suggests that the new mines should house whole families in villages rather than house male workers in crowded compounds. Money is not everything, the voice says, and the world does not need a second Johannesburg.

SUMMARY — CHAPTER 24

Jarvis returns to Arthur's house and finds an article entitled "Private Essay on the Evolution of a South African." In it, Arthur writes that he had an idyllic childhood and was raised by parents who taught him about honor, charity, and generosity. They taught him nothing, however, of South Africa. Jarvis is so hurt and angered by this statement that he almost leaves the house. At the last minute, he stops and returns to the essay. Arthur explains that he will now devote himself to truth and justice in his country, not because he is especially courageous, but because he wishes to be released from the contradictions that mar his everyday life. He no longer wants to be idealistic in some parts of his life and self-protective in others. He hopes that his children will come to feel as he feels. Jarvis is moved and sits thinking for a long time. He eventually gets up to leave, and the narrator notes that the bloodstained back passageway where Arthur was killed holds no power over Jarvis now. Jarvis leaves from the front door.

ANALYSIS — BOOK II: CHAPTERS 22–24

Absalom's testimony adds religious overtones to the actions surrounding Arthur Jarvis's murder. The "voice" that tells Johannes when the robbery should be committed and the allegedly "blessed" nature of the iron rod, for example, suggest that Johannes, at least, thinks of the robbery as divine retribution for the inequalities that plague blacks. Absalom, however, is uncomfortable with the violent and superstitious nature of Johannes's claims. Though he gets involved in the un-Christian act of robbery, he does so not to harm someone else but for gain; he seems slightly less immoral than Johannes. Furthermore, Absalom reverts to his Christian teachings after the murder. Unlike Johannes and Matthew, who do everything they can to escape blame, Absalom prays for forgiveness after he buries the weapon. He accepts his guilt and even confesses, knowing that he has done wrong.

The return of the unidentified and impersonal narrative voice in Chapter 23 to announce the discovery of gold in Odendaalsrust reflects white South Africa's skewed priorities. The mines are a powerful but understated presence up to this point in the novel, but here Paton thrusts them into the foreground to highlight their role in creating the tension between the issue of white wealth and black poverty. The news of these new gold mines completely eclipses news of the Arthur Jarvis murder trial, demonstrating that white South Africa, in general, cares much more about wealth than about its dire race problems. This discovery of gold makes grown men weep or sing about the performance of gold stocks, and these greedy whites prefer to ignore the inequalities created by the racist system that benefits them so much. Instead, they focus on the power of money, which can create a whole city where there is only grass and dirt.

This narrator also implies that power and wealth are not simply issues of white versus black. There are also political and social differences between South Africa's English inhabitants and its Afrikaners. The grumblings over the name of the mine seem to imply that the Afrikaners are a major presence in the mines and that the English would rather they not be. The voice also brings up the issue of the bilingual state and remarks wistfully how much easier it would be if the Afrikaners would simply accept English as the nation's language. Clearly, black Africans are not the only South Africans whose culture is being targeted. But though the English dislike Afrikaans, they do tolerate the language and consider it South Africa's second language. They utterly dismiss, on the other hand, native African tongues such as Zulu and Xosa.

In Chapter 24, the character of Arthur Jarvis is resurrected through his essay on his personal evolution. Until now, while certainly an admirable figure, Jarvis has been a figure of passion and politics, but without much personality. This essay, however, allows for some real communication from son to father, an experience so intense that the older Jarvis almost flees the room. Eventually, however, James Jarvis forces himself to read his son's essay, and in doing so, he takes the first step in fulfilling his recent wish to know his son better. While father and son often disagreed in life, Arthur's writings offer his father some comfort from the grave.

BOOK II: CHAPTERS 25–27

> *That man should walk upright in the land where they were born . . . what was there evil in it? . . . such fear could not be cast out, but by love.*
>
> (See QUOTATIONS, p. 69)

SUMMARY — CHAPTER 25

Jarvis and his wife go to visit one of Mrs. Jarvis's favorite nieces, Barbara Smith. While the women go into town, Jarvis stays behind to read the newspaper's reports on crime and the gold rush. There is a knock at the door, and when Jarvis opens it, he is surprised to see a frail black parson in tattered clothes. The parson seems shocked by the sight of Jarvis and begins trembling so much that he is forced to sit down on the house steps. Torn between compassion and irritation, Jarvis holds the parson's stick and hat while the parson struggles to his feet and collects his scattered papers.

The parson explains that he is there to check on a friend's daughter who had come to work for the household. Jarvis refers him to the house's native servant, then realizes that the man before him must be the parson, known in Zulu as the "umfundisi," of Ndotsheni, Jarvis's hometown. Jarvis tells the parson that he may wait for the mistress of the house to return, then asks the old man why he is so afraid of him. The umfundisi, who does not give his name but is obviously Kumalo, reveals that it is his son who murdered Arthur Jarvis. Jarvis leaves abruptly to walk around the garden, and though he is obviously very emotional when he returns, he informs the parson that he is not angry. They share a memory of Arthur when he was young, and Kumalo tells Jarvis how saddened he is by the Jarvis family's loss. Mrs. Smith returns and curtly informs Kumalo, through Jarvis, that the girl he seeks was fired after she was arrested for distilling liquor. She has no idea where the girl is now, although Jarvis does not translate this last statement. The parson leaves, and when Mrs. Jarvis asks Jarvis why he seems disturbed, Jarvis makes a cryptic comment about a visit from the past.

SUMMARY — CHAPTER 26

John Kumalo addresses a crowd with his powerful voice. His voice rolls out beautifully, like thunder, but his comrades Dubula and Tomlinson listen with scorn and envy, for it is a powerful voice not backed by their courage or intelligence. John argues that the wealth from the new gold that has been found in South Africa should be shared with the miners. The crowd roars with John as he declares that the miners deserve higher wages and better conditions. Some of the white policemen on guard say that John should be shot or imprisoned. The narrator notes that while some leaders want to go to prison as martyrs, John does not, since he knows that in prison there is no applause. Toward the end of his speech, he states that he and the crowd do not want to trouble the police.

Stephen Kumalo and Msimangu are among the listeners. Kumalo is impressed, but Msimangu is skeptical—he knows that

John lacks courage, and wonders why God should have given this man a gift of such oratorical skill. Still, he is thankful that John lacks heart, because he believes that if John backed up his words with action, he could plunge the country into violence and bloodshed. They move forward to hear the next speaker, Tomlinson. Jarvis and John Harrison, who have also been at the meeting, leave for Harrison's club. Jarvis refuses to discuss what he has just seen, simply stating that he does not "care for that sort of thing."

A police captain reports to his officer. He states that John Kumalo is dangerous and comments on the power of his voice. The officer comments on Kumalo's voice as well, saying that he must go hear it one day. The captain wonders if there will be a strike. The officer replies that a strike could be a "nasty business."

The narrative voice returns and states that there are rumors that the strike may spread to the railroads and the ships. The narrator adds that such a terrible prospect makes some white people think about how much they depend on black labor.

In the end, an anonymous voice tells us, the strike amounts to very little. There is some trouble at the mines, and three black miners are killed, but the strike never spreads. A clergyman at one of the nation's religious conferences brings up the issue of black laborers, but, the voice notes, it's easier not to think about such things. The voice restates that the strike is over and notes that everything is quiet. Even in the most serene place, a voice retorts, there is no silence. Only fools are quiet.

SUMMARY — CHAPTER 27

Mrs. Lithebe again reprimands Gertrude for talking and laughing carelessly. Gertrude is defensive and upset, and Mrs. Lithebe tells Gertrude that she does not understand the ways of decent people. Gertrude faults Johannesburg for her corruption and says she will be glad to be gone. Meanwhile, a neighbor brings a newspaper that announces that another white man has been murdered during a break-in by a native. The neighbor and Mrs. Lithebe worry that the news will hurt Absalom's case. Msimangu arrives, and he and Mrs. Lithebe decide to hide the paper from Kumalo. To prevent Kumalo from hearing the news, they eat dinner at Mrs. Lithebe's instead of at the mission.

Afterward, the group goes to church and listens to a woman describe her decision to become a nun. Later that night, Gertrude suggests to Mrs. Lithebe that she might become a nun. Mrs. Lithebe is pleased by the impulse, and says it warrants further thought. Gertrude asks Absalom's girlfriend if she will look after Gertrude's son if Gertrude becomes a nun, and the girl agrees. Gertrude makes Absalom's girlfriend promise to keep Gertrude's idea a secret until it is final, but Gertrude hopes out loud that this decision will keep her from her careless lifestyle.

ANALYSIS — BOOK II: CHAPTERS 25–27

Chapter 25 proves to be a pivotal meeting point for the novel's two main perspectives. Book I follows Kumalo, and until this point, Book II has largely been told from Jarvis's point of view. In Chapter 25, the two men finally meet, and their stories intersect. Paton's decision to narrate their meeting from Jarvis's point of view gives us a new perspective on the story. This narrative structure puts us in Jarvis's shoes. When Jarvis answers the door and finds Kumalo, we are told only that a frail black parson is there. Though we quickly realize that this man must be Kumalo, we share Jarvis's confusion and suspense until Kumalo identifies himself several pages later. This distance between the two characters mirrors the distance between South Africa's white and black populations in general. Seeing things from Jarvis's point of view also gives us a new perspective on Kumalo. Having seen Kumalo's quest for his son through Kumalo's eyes, we do not realize what a physical toll this search has taken until Jarvis notices how weak Kumalo is. We also more fully understand Kumalo's grief for what his son has done because we see how much encountering Jarvis upsets him. Paton makes these two stories intersect in a manner that reinforces not only the distance between whites and blacks but also the nature of their conflict—that blacks are weak and powerless whereas whites are strong and powerful.

Jarvis struggles with a conflict between his conservative perspective that "natives" do not deserve the same considerations as white people, a belief exemplified by Barbara Smith's curt dismissal of Kumalo's inquiry about his friend's daughter, and his desire to extend compassion and courtesy to a frail old man. This split attitude helps explain Jarvis's interaction with Kumalo at the door. He picks up Kumalo's walking stick when Kumalo drops it, but he becomes "torn between compassion and irritation" when Kumalo accidentally drops a bunch of papers. When Kumalo explains to Jarvis, however, that "the heaviest thing of all my years, is the heaviest thing of all your years also," Jarvis seems to understand that the grief the men share puts them on common ground. What differentiates Jarvis from whites such as Barbara Smith, then, is his ability to empathize and identify with others regardless of skin color.

Chapter 26 is a meditation on the complicated relationship between words and social change. John Kumalo speaks beautifully, but he does not demand radical change in the circumstances facing the black population. As Msimangu explains, John is too attached to his own possessions and social position to put himself in real danger. This episode raises some interesting questions about Paton's views on the merit of words versus action. We see the power of words in the eloquent writings of Arthur Jarvis, and it never occurs to us to question their honesty and ability to change things. With John Kumalo, however, we begin to see that simple eloquence is not enough to bring about social change. The same can be said for unfocused action as well, as can be seen in the easy put down of the strike. With these examples, the novel argues that social protest does not have meaning without the good intentions and methodical planning necessary to see it through.

BOOK II: CHAPTERS 28–29

SUMMARY — CHAPTER 28

The judge delivers his verdict on Absalom's crime. While a Zulu interpreter translates, the judge explains that even though Arthur's servant identified Johannes as having been present during the break-in, there is not enough proof to convict Johannes. Although he acknowledges that Absalom's testimony is vivid and that it was corroborated by plenty of circumstantial evidence, the judge also wonders out loud whether Absalom named his accomplices to alleviate his own guilt. For these reasons, the judge declares Johannes and Matthew not guilty, although he hopes there will be further investigation into their previous criminal activities.

The judge turns his attention to Absalom. He agrees with many of Mr. Carmichael's arguments regarding Absalom's remorse, the honesty of his testimony, and his youth. He also mentions Carmichael's argument that the destruction of tribal society and the conditions of native life in Johannesburg contributed to the crime. The judge explains, however, that he must uphold the law, even if that law was made by an unjust society. If Absalom had truly fired in fear, the judge says, the charge of murder would have to be dropped, but he says the fact that Absalom brought a loaded revolver into the house and that the servant was struck with an iron bar demonstrate an intention to kill. Therefore, he finds Absalom guilty of murder. The judge believes there are no special grounds for mercy, which means that Absalom is sentenced to hang. Only the governor-general-in-council can lessen Absalom's sentence. The young man from the reformatory, who has attended the trial, crosses the color line that separates whites and blacks in the courtroom in order to help Kumalo exit.

SUMMARY — CHAPTER 29

Father Vincent, Kumalo, Gertrude, Msimangu, and Absalom's girl-friend go to the prison so that Absalom can be married. After the marriage, Absalom and his father have a final meeting. Absalom sends his remembrances to his mother and directs his father to his last savings and possessions, which will help with the upkeep of his son. Kumalo bitterly mentions that he finds it hard to forgive Matthew and Johannes for abandoning Absalom. The time comes for Absalom to be taken away, and he begins to weep because he is afraid of dying. Two guards have to pull Absalom from his father's knees when it is time for Kumalo to leave. Outside, Absalom's girl-friend joyfully greets Kumalo as her father, but he is too distracted to pay much attention to her.

Kumalo goes to say good-bye to his brother. After some tense pleasantries, John tells Kumalo that he intends to bring Matthew back to his shop once the trouble has passed. Kumalo asks John where his politics are taking him. John replies that Kumalo should not interfere with his politics since he does not interfere with Kumalo's religion. Kumalo warns John that his words may get him in trouble with the police, and when he sees fear in his brother's eyes, Kumalo presses further in order to hurt John. Kumalo lies and says that he has heard that a spy has come to John's shop and has been reporting on the secret conversations John conducts there. When John shakes his head at the thought of being betrayed by a friend, Kumalo angrily cries out that his son had two such friends. John drives him from the store, and Kumalo walks away, distressed that he has failed in his mission to warn John against the corrupting influence of power.

The Jarvises bid their farewell to the Harrisons, who agree with the sentencing and wish the other two men had been convicted as well. Jarvis agrees. At the station, Jarvis slips John Harrison an envelope containing a check for a thousand pounds for the boys' club that John and Arthur founded.

There is a farewell gathering for Kumalo at Mrs. Lithebe's house. Msimangu tells Kumalo that he has decided to renounce all of his possessions and become a monk. He gives Kumalo his savings, over thirty-three pounds—more money than Kumalo has ever possessed. Kumalo falls to his knees in amazement and decides to send John a letter to apologize for his actions. The following morning, he wakes Absalom's wife for the journey to Ndotsheni. In Gertrude's room, however, he finds her son and her clothes neatly laid out, but Gertrude is gone.

Analysis — Book II: Chapters 28–29

The judge's sentencing of Absalom demonstrates that white South Africa's concern lies in self-preservation rather than in progress toward racial equality. Though he toys with the notion that the question of justice in Absalom's case must take into account the condition of society as a whole, the judge ends up pinning responsibility for the crime on Absalom. By shifting his focus from the larger picture of how society influences individuals to the smaller picture of how Absalom acted in a particular instant, the judge reinforces a truth about the society in which he lives: reason and compassion cannot triumph over ingrained prejudice. The judge is sympathetic to Absalom's situation, but he proves himself a slave to the legal system, stating that despite his feelings he must act in accordance with the laws. By acknowledging the potential unfairness of these laws but refusing to undermine them further, the judge dehumanizes black South Africans. Finally, he ignores the fact that white South Africa oppresses black South Africans when he argues that South Africa's ability to abide by its laws in the face of social upheaval is a sign of hope for the country.

The novel spends little time dealing with the various characters' reactions to Absalom's sentence, suggesting that any debate over Absalom's guilt is irrelevant. Absalom reacts as we expect someone in his situation would react—with fear. Kumalo barely even addresses the sentencing. The family members of the victim find solace in the conviction in proportion to their dislike of blacks: the more conservative Mr. Harrison is pleased but wishes the other two youths had been convicted as well, while the more moderate Jarvis limits his comments on the matter to agreeing with Harrison's support of the sentencing. Paton mutes his characters' reactions to Absalom's sentence perhaps to show how little impact people can have on the South African system. No amount of individual emotion, it seems, can sway such institutionalized values.

The conflict between John and Kumalo is also exposed here, and though the brothers have grown distant over the years, in Chapter 29 their separation becomes final. In this scene, however, John is less despicable than in previous passages. He plans to welcome Matthew back into his house, and he draws an interesting comparison between his brother's religion and his own politics. Perhaps, this chapter suggests, Kumalo's religion is as offensive to John as John's politics are to Kumalo. Although the novel has always depicted John as nothing more than a bull-necked rabble-rouser, for a fleeting instant we see the situation through his eyes: a man tired of the indignities suffered by his people, with no time for the meek protests of his brother. That the novel sides with Kumalo is clear, but its inherent sense of justice also compels us to look for a brief moment at a conflict from the offending party's point of view.

BOOK III: CHAPTERS 30–33

SUMMARY — CHAPTER 30

The trains carry Kumalo, Absalom's wife, and Gertrude's son back to Ndotsheni. They are greeted warmly, and Kumalo's wife refers to the young girl as her daughter. As they walk to Kumalo's home, they encounter people from the village who tell Kumalo how happy they are to have their *umfundisi* back. They confess that they are worried about the drought that is starving their crops. A friend tells Kumalo that the Jarvises have returned and that the villagers are aware of what Absalom has done.

When Kumalo arrives at his church, he finds a gathering of followers already assembled, and he leads them in a prayer. He asks for rain, for the welcome of Absalom's wife and Gertrude's son, and for forgiveness for Gertrude and Absalom. After the service, he speaks with his friend from the railroad station. Kumalo tells his friend all about Gertrude and Absalom. He says that since the news will soon be known, his friend should spread the word. Kumalo worries that he is too disgraced to lead his congregation, but his friend assures him otherwise. When his friend asks about Sibeko's daughter,

Kumalo tells his friend that the girl is lost. Kumalo comes home in time to wish Absalom's wife goodnight, then sits up with his wife discussing Msimangu's gift and other, sadder matters.

SUMMARY — CHAPTER 31
Kumalo prays that his village can be restored. He visits the village chief, but he cannot share in the chief's optimism, as it is all too clear that the white men made the chiefs powerless and left mere figureheads in their place. The chief shares Kumalo's concern about the departure of the young people of the village for Johannesburg but has no new ideas about how to change things, and he concludes the interview by sadly resolving to try to bring these issues up with the local magistrate once more. Kumalo visits the school headmaster, but he fears that the headmaster's teachings about farming are more academic than practical. He considers them pleasant theories that do not prevent the valley from drying up and its children from dying.

As Kumalo mulls over his disappointments, Arthur's son rides by on horseback. He is staying with his grandfather. He greets Kumalo with uncustomary politeness and asks to see his home. The boy asks for a drink of milk, but there is no milk in Ndotsheni. He asks what children do without milk, and Kumalo tells him that some children are dying. The small boy practices his Zulu with Kumalo and rides off.

That evening, a worker from Jarvis's farm delivers milk to be given to all of the small children in Ndotsheni. Overwhelmed by the suddenness of this gift, Kumalo laughs until he is sore.

SUMMARY — CHAPTER 32
Four letters are delivered to Kumalo's household. One, from Mr. Carmichael, explains that Absalom will not be given mercy and will be hanged that month. Another is from Absalom. Kumalo and his wife read this letter together. Absalom writes that he is comfortable in the Pretoria prison and is being ministered to by a priest, but he knows now that he must die. He writes simply and directly about his life in prison and states that he now understands that he belongs in Ndotsheni. The third letter is from Absalom for his wife. The fourth letter is from Msimangu, and when Kumalo reads Msimangu's descriptions of Johannesburg, he is surprised to find himself missing the city.

Meanwhile, the long-awaited storm that will break the drought rolls in. Kumalo sees Jarvis and the local magistrate drive into Ndotsheni and plant some sticks with flags. The chief is charged with making sure that no one tampers with the flags. After commenting that Jarvis is rumored to be both mad and bankrupt, the magistrate leaves, while Jarvis stays behind to measure the land. When the storm comes, he seeks shelter in Kumalo's church. The two sit together under Kumalo's leaky roof, and Jarvis asks whether Absalom has received mercy. Kumalo shows him the letter from Mr. Carmichael, and Jarvis says that he understands Kumalo's grief. When the storm passes, the residents of Ndotsheni examine the sticks with great curiosity. When a child uproots one, there is much commotion, and the whole village conspires to put the stick back in its place and conceal all evidence of its removal.

SUMMARY — CHAPTER 33

It is rumored that the sticks mark the place were a dam will be built in Ndotsheni. Absalom's wife and Gertrude's son settle rapidly into their new home. Arthur's son comes to visit Kumalo again and practice his Zulu. He tells Kumalo that he will return to Johannesburg when his grandfather comes back from Pietermaritzburg, and Kumalo comments that Ndotsheni will lose something bright when the boy leaves. Kumalo teaches Arthur's son some new Zulu words and explains their origins. When Kumalo's wife joins them, the boy surprises her with his command of the language.

Arthur's son sees Jarvis's car climbing the hill and gallops eagerly after it to welcome his grandfather home. A young black man comes to Kumalo's church and introduces himself to Kumalo. His name is Napoleon Letsitsi, and he is an agricultural expert hired by Jarvis to teach better farming techniques. He agrees to stay with the Kumalos while he helps to recover the valley. It will be difficult, Letsitsi says, because he will have to teach the people that their land must be farmed for the common good, not for each individual's best interests. Hardest of all, he says, will be convincing people to stop measuring their wealth in cattle, as cattle damage the land and do not allow it to recover. Letsitsi confirms that a dam is being built. Arthur's son returns to say good-bye to Kumalo. He promises to continue his Zulu lessons during his holidays.

ANALYSIS — BOOK III: CHAPTERS 30–33

In the aftermath of Absalom's conviction for murder, Paton creates a fragile balance of despair and hope in Kumalo's life. Kumalo is saddened and frustrated by the devastation of Ndotsheni, which has been further worsened by the drought, and neither the chief nor the school headmaster knows how the area can be mended. Furthermore, Kumalo receives the news that there will be no mercy for his son. Thus, on one hand, both land and family—two important elements of Kumalo's life—are sources of grief. He is given hope, however, by the friendliness and curiosity of Arthur's son, by Jarvis's gift of milk to the community, and by the agricultural improvements that Jarvis attempts to make. Furthermore, the rain eventually comes and ends the drought. Absalom's letter continues the reconciliation between father and son. Here, then, land and family become sources of happiness, suggesting that Kumalo's misfortunes, though they are grave, will not last forever.

The improvements planned for Ndotsheni will, however, forever alter the village's way of life by imposing European methods of farming, and Paton constantly underscores the foreignness of the proposed methods. At first, Jarvis's activities are mysterious to the villagers, and they view the flags as a curiosity. The native chief is relegated to guard duty while Jarvis and the magistrate fulfill the far more important duty of planting the flags and planning the project, which demonstrates the distance that still exists between the white farmers and the local community. Napoleon Letsitsi explains that the agricultural improvements will require sacrifices on the part of the villagers as well, effectively devaluating their whole cattle-as-currency system and their concept of farming as an individual activity. Nonetheless, it seems evident that the people of Ndotsheni will come to accept these changes. Although they are curious about the flags, they treat them with great respect, and the whole community gathers to replant the uprooted flag.

Arthur's son emerges as a bridge between these separate worlds. Jarvis has a good heart, but he makes little or no effort to socialize with the villagers of Ndotsheni. Arthur's son strides into Kumalo's house without fear. Though only a child, he has already begun to learn Zulu. His eagerness to speak Zulu shows a lack of concern for the superficial racial divisions of South African society. Most telling of all, however, is that the boy and Kumalo laugh together. When Jarvis and Kumalo meet in Kumalo's church during the storm, it is still a formal affair, and though the two men come to respect each other, their ultimate goal seems to be coexistence. With his Zulu lessons and his jokes, Arthur's son crosses the final line and opens up the possibility of actual friendship between whites and blacks.

BOOK III: CHAPTERS 34–36

SUMMARY — CHAPTER 34

As Kumalo and his congregation prepare for a confirmation cere-
mony at the church, one of Jarvis's workers brings word that
Jarvis's wife, Margaret, has died. As the women lament, Kumalo
writes a letter of condolence to Jarvis in which he mentions that he
suspects that Margaret is partly responsible for the great contribu-
tions Jarvis is making to the village. He questions whether to send it,
wondering whether Arthur's murder is somehow the cause of the
sickness that killed her. He decides, however, that Jarvis is a man
who stays by the path he has chosen, and sends the letter.

At the confirmation, rain leaks through the roof of the church
and onto the congregation. Afterward, Kumalo and the Bishop meet
privately. The Bishop thinks that Kumalo should leave Ndotsheni
because his son killed Jarvis's son, and because Absalom's wife
became pregnant out of wedlock. He has found a position for
Kumalo where no one will know of these things. Kumalo is crushed
but swallows the bishop's arguments and obeys. As he and the
Bishop are talking, however, a timely letter arrives. Jarvis has written back, thanking Kumalo for his sympathy and assuring him that
Arthur's murder had nothing to do with his wife's illness. He wants
to build a new church for Ndotsheni. Elated, Kumalo shows the letter to the Bishop, and the Bishop agrees that it is God's will for
Kumalo to stay in Ndotsheni. Kumalo comes home to find his wife
and other church members hard at work on a sympathy wreath for
the Jarvis family. He sends a local man to gather the appropriate
flowers for a white man's wreath.

SUMMARY — CHAPTER 35

Napoleon Letsitsi, the agricultural expert, teaches the people new
ways to plow. He plans to build a *kraal*, where the cattle will be
kept. The villagers work with new spirit, but the ones who have had
to give up their land are sullen. The future, Letsitsi tells Kumalo, will
hold even bigger changes, and he hopes that the people will see the
need for these changes themselves and not have to be convinced.

Kumalo praises Letsitsi, but Letsitsi is worried that it will take
time for great improvements to happen. Letsitsi also speaks eagerly
of the time when the people will not need to take the white man's
milk but will instead be able to provide milk of their own. Kumalo

is disturbed by this sentiment, but Letsitsi is insistent. He is grateful to Jarvis, he says, and to other good white men, but though they pay his salary, he works for Africa and not for them. It is the white man's policies that have made such improvements necessary, he says, and these efforts are only repayment for a debt long overdue. Letsitsi assures Kumalo, however, that he is not there to make trouble. Kumalo gives Letsitsi a final warning about hatred and power and is glad to see that the young man is interested in neither. Kumalo stands for a minute gazing at the stars and reflecting that these new, radical politics have come too late for him. There are some who might call him a white man's dog, Kumalo thinks, but it is the way he has lived, and he has done with it what he can.

SUMMARY — CHAPTER 36

Kumalo has a place he goes to contemplate the weightier things in life, and on the night before Absalom is to die, he travels to this mountaintop to keep vigil. On the way, he meets Jarvis, who informs him that plans for the new church will arrive shortly. Jarvis thanks Kumalo for the sympathy wreath. They speak of Arthur's son, then reminisce about Arthur himself. Jarvis asks where Kumalo is going, and when Kumalo replies, he says that he understands. Kumalo thanks Jarvis for all he has done for the village and tells Jarvis that he has been touched by God.

In his place of solitude, Kumalo goes over Absalom's letters from prison, in which Absalom assures him that if he could return to Ndotsheni, he would. Kumalo repents for his own sins and gives thanks for the many blessings he has received during his time of trouble. He wakes up and turns his mind to the suffering of others—the missing Gertrude, the people of Shanty Town, his own wife, and above all, Absalom. Kumalo reflects on the plight of Africa and on Msimangu's whispered fear that by the time the white man learns to love, the black man will have learned to hate. He sleeps and wakes up just before dawn, wondering what his son, who will be hanged when the sun rises, is doing at that moment. The light rises, and the narrator wonders when the light of emancipation will come to the forsaken land of South Africa.

ANALYSIS — BOOK III: CHAPTERS 34–36

In their final encounters, Kumalo and Jarvis become the closest they have ever been. They have slowly begun to understand each other's customs and to communicate through gestures and words that each can understand. When Margaret Jarvis dies, Kumalo's congregation mourns the death with the European custom of crafting a wreath. When Jarvis meets Kumalo as he climbs to a place of solitude, he greets the information with a solemn statement of understanding. Until now, the two men have been armed with good intentions but have failed to cross the lines into each other's world. The imbalanced power dynamic between whites and blacks is still very much in play: Jarvis sits atop his horse while Kumalo humbly thanks him. Nevertheless, the intense moment of understanding and compassion that they share is perhaps a slight step toward bridging the country's enormous racial divide.

Absalom too comes to embody this idea that sometimes understanding one's situation is enough. The last time we encounter Absalom, in Chapter 29, he is groveling in the prison in front of his father, being drawn away to his cell on death row without any trace of dignity. His letters from prison since Kumalo's departure, however, reflect an increasing peace that comes with his understanding his circumstances. He does not protest against his fate; rather, he deals with it as maturely as possible, perhaps taking solace in the notion that he is but a small part of a large universe that works in mysterious ways. It is not clear that Absalom is entirely reconciled to his fate—Kumalo wonders if his son can sleep and if he will enjoy his last meal—but Absalom's letters imply a newfound peace of mind, which is something valuable in the turbulence of the times.

The final paragraph ends with the breaking of the dawn, but in many ways the novel ends with a sunset. Absalom, Arthur Jarvis, and Margaret Jarvis are all dead, and neither James Jarvis nor Kumalo will live much longer. Paton implies that their legacy of peace will not endure. A newer, more fiery school of thought is on the rise, and the redemption present in the novel's conclusion will not prevent this radical approach from eventually dominating the country. Napoleon Letsitsi is not as corrupt as John Kumalo, but he still argues fiercely for black self-sufficiency and views Jarvis's last gestures toward Ndotsheni as the payment of a debt rather than an act of generosity. As Kumalo stands outside his house, gazing at the stars, he becomes aware that this change is inevitable and that history may even view him as an impediment to this change. He does take some consolation, however, in knowing that his life has been the only kind he could possibly have led and hopes that the changes for the better will outpace the changes for the worse.

IMPORTANT QUOTATIONS EXPLAINED

1. The white man has broken the tribe. And it is my belief—and again I ask your pardon—that it cannot be mended again. But the house that is broken, and the man that falls apart when the house is broken, these are the tragic things. That is why children break the law, and old white people are robbed and beaten.

Msimangu makes this statement in Chapter 5 after he welcomes Kumalo to Johannesburg, while discussing the troubles of Gertrude and Absalom. Msimangu explains to Kumalo what he believes has gone wrong with their country: the tribal bonds have been broken, giving young men and women no reason to stay in their villages. These youths then go to Johannesburg, where they inevitably lose their way and become morally corrupt. Msimangu is very explicit about the cause-and-effect relationship that he perceives between the deterioration of black culture and crime against whites. As such, he expresses the novel's central preoccupation with the matter of tribal structure and its important role in holding the country's black population together.

QUOTATIONS

2.   I see only one hope for our country, and that is when white men and black men . . . desiring only the good of their country, come together to work for it. . . . I have one great fear in my heart, that one day when they are turned to loving, they will find we are turned to hating.

Msimangu speaks these words in Chapter 7 immediately after he and Kumalo meet with John. Msimangu doubts John's convictions, and instead of calling him a champion of justice, Msimangu calls John an example of power's corrupting influence. Msimangu warns that power can corrupt black people as much as it corrupts white people. It is exactly this corruption that keeps South Africa in its predicament, and in this passage Msimangu unveils his dream of a selfless Christian faith that will bind all people—black and white—together.

Msimangu's fear that by the time "they"—the whites—turn to loving, "we"—the blacks—will have turned to hating calls attention to Kumalo's sense of the shift in black attitudes toward whites. Although Kumalo and Msimangu, members of an older generation, do not wish to cause strife, younger men such as Napoleon Letsitsi are less willing to tolerate white oppression. The willingness to be reconciled exists among both blacks and whites, Msimangu suggests, but never at the same time. Through Msimangu, Paton hints at the sad irony of a nation in which justice and racial equality are stymied by poor timing rather than bad intentions.

3. This is no time to talk of hedges and fields, or the
    beauties of any country. . . . Cry for the broken tribe,
    for the law and the custom that is gone. Aye, and cry
    aloud for the man who is dead, for the woman and
    children bereaved. Cry, the beloved country, these
    things are not yet at an end.

This quotation, from Chapter 11, stands in contrast to the novel's
early tendency to dwell on the lush South African landscape and
urges sorrow instead. By breaking out of this pattern and address-
ing us with such urgency, the narrator reflects how grave and
ingrained South Africa's problems are. The quotation's ominous
last line is a note of prophetic foreshadowing of Absalom's death,
and though it certainly reflects the pessimism Kumalo and his
brethren may feel, it also informs us that this episode is one of
many blows that South Africa has yet to endure.

QUOTATIONS

4. The truth is that our civilization is not Christian; it is a
    tragic compound of great ideal and fearful practice, of
    high assurance and desperate anxiety, of loving charity
    and fearful clutching of possessions. Allow me a
    minute. . . .

These words are written by Arthur Jarvis and read by his father in
Chapter 21. Arthur contrasts a Christianity that supports the
notion of black people as inferior with a true Christianity that
rejects white superiority. Some Christians, Arthur says, argue that it
is God's will that black South Africans remain unskilled workers.
Trying to educate them would be an un-Christian action, and therefore wrong. Arthur argues, however, that every human being has the
right to develop his or her God-given gifts. Because South Africa
ignores this principle, Arthur argues, it is not a truly Christian state.

  The cut-off sentence that closes Arthur's statement is especially
poignant for his father, as these are the last words that Arthur writes
before going downstairs to his death. Ironically, Arthur Jarvis is on
the verge of envisioning a new South Africa when the problems of
the old one cut him down. This tragic turn of events indicates the
dire need for change.

5. And now for all the people of Africa, the beloved country. *Nkosi Sikelel' iAfrika,* God save Africa. But he would not see that salvation. It lay afar off, because men were afraid of it. Because, to tell the truth, they were afraid of him, and his wife, and Msimangu, and the young demonstrator. And what was there evil in their desires, in their hunger? That man should walk upright in the land where they were born, and be free to use the fruits of the earth, what was there evil in it? . . . They were afraid because they were so few. And such fear could not be cast out, but by love.

These thoughts are part of the novel's conclusion, as Kumalo keeps his vigil on the mountain while Absalom hangs. Kumalo prays for Africa, even though he knows it will be a long time before his prayers are answered. He understands that fear is the root of injustice: white men fear black men because there are so few whites and so many blacks. They worry that if the basic needs of the black population are met, then there will be little left for them. Kumalo observes, however, that there is nothing evil in him or his desires, or in his people's desire for a better life. They want simply their due as humans (to "walk upright" and "use the fruits of the earth"). They are not motivated by hatred and revenge, but by a simple desire for dignity. Kumalo's rumination ends with a somewhat troubling paradox: for whites to stop being afraid, they must begin to understand and then love; in order to understand and then love, however, they must stop being afraid. It thus seems impossible for whites and blacks to exist as equals.

QUOTATIONS

Key Facts

FULL TITLE

Cry, the Beloved Country

AUTHOR

Alan Paton

TYPE OF WORK

Novel

GENRE

Father's quest for his son; courtroom drama; social criticism

LANGUAGE

English

TIME AND PLACE WRITTEN

Various parts of Europe and the United States, in 1946

DATE OF FIRST PUBLICATION

1948

PUBLISHER

Charles Scribner

NARRATOR

The third-person narrator is omniscient, or all-knowing, and temporarily inhabits many different points of view.

POINT OF VIEW

Books I and III are largely told from Kumalo's point of view, while Book II is told largely from Jarvis's point of view. A number of chapters, however, feature a montage of voices from different layers of South African society, and the narrator also shows things from other characters' perspectives from time to time.

TONE

Lyrical, grieving, elegiac, occasionally bitter

TENSE

Past

SETTING (TIME)
Mid-1940s, just after World War II

SETTING (PLACE)
Ndotsheni and Johannesburg, South Africa

PROTAGONIST
Stephen Kumalo; James Jarvis

MAJOR CONFLICT
Stephen Kumalo struggles against the forces (white oppression, the corrupting influences of city life) that destroy his family and his country

RISING ACTION
Kumalo travels to Johannesburg to search for his son

CLIMAX
Absalom is arrested for the murder of Arthur Jarvis

FALLING ACTION
Absalom is sentenced to death; Jarvis works with Kumalo to improve conditions in the village; Absalom is hanged

THEMES
Separation and reconciliation between fathers and sons; the impact of social injustice on individuals; crime and punishment; Christian love as a response to injustice

MOTIFS
Descriptions of nature; anger and repentance; repeated phrases

SYMBOLS
The church, brightness, sunrise

FORESHADOWING
When Kumalo sees in the newspaper that a white man has been killed by native South Africans during a break-in, he has a premonition that Absalom is involved.

KEY FACTS

STUDY QUESTIONS & ESSAY TOPICS

STUDY QUESTIONS

1. *Msimangu says that the main problem facing the native population of South Africa is that nothing has been built to replace the broken moral and social framework of the tribes. John Kumalo thinks the main trouble is economic inequality. Based on the evidence in the novel, which of these men is right?*

It is impossible to separate economic inequality and the breakdown of the tribal way of life fully, because to a large degree, economic inequality is responsible for this breakdown. The land can no longer support the people, so the young men and women migrate to the morally corrupted cities. In this sense, both men are right. But Msimangu has a better grasp of the complexity of the problems gripping South Africa and a more attractive vision of what a better South Africa may look like. John seems to believe that black people simply need more money and power to be free. Msimangu, however, envisions freedom as the right to live in a moral and just society, not as power and possessions. He would like to see South Africa built on a foundation of selfless love rather than personal self-interest. Without a moral framework and new traditions to give life meaning, he believes, money and power will bring little happiness. John's vision of life lacks a commitment to family and high ideals and is therefore essentially empty.

2. *What is the role of Christianity—a European religion embraced by most of the natives, including Kumalo—in* Cry, the Beloved Country? *Why has it not succeeded in improving the moral framework of the tribal system?*

Christianity is central to Kumalo's character and his understanding of the world. It is his Christian faith that allows him to bear the hardships that he faces. If everyone in South Africa embraced the Christian ideals of brotherly love, forgiveness, and charity, then perhaps Christianity could succeed in replacing the broken tribal system. Some whites in South Africa, however, use Christianity to rationalize injustice. They claim that God wants the blacks to remain unskilled and lacking power. In this way, Christianity becomes part of South Africa's problems instead of a potential solution. Kumalo's Christianity seems to blend tribal values and Christian values, which overlap a good deal. He calls God "Tixo," an African word for the Great Spirit, and the tribal ideas about the importance of the family are indistinguishable from Christian ones. It would seem that true Christianity is as threatened by the injustices of South Africa as the old tribal structure once was.

3.   *What role does the landscape play in the novel? What*
     does the valley surrounding Ndotsheni seem to represent?

The landscape surrounding Ndotsheni represents the basic good-ness and beauty of Africa. This land can nourish and sustain a large number of people and give them great happiness. In Ndotsheni itself, however, the land is not so beautiful. It has been damaged by over-grazing and poor farming techniques. Lacking education and restricted to limited plots of land, the villagers of Ndotsheni injure the land because they have not been taught to protect it and because too many of them are competing for the same resources. The beauty of South Africa, it would seem, depends upon the justice and wis-dom of the social systems it supports. If these systems are ugly, then the land will come to mirror them. South Africa's beauty is a source of hope, but this hope must be carefully protected and nurtured. Jarvis's attempt, at the end of the novel, to teach the people of Ndot-sheni better farming techniques is a step in this direction.

SUGGESTED ESSAY TOPICS

1. One of the novel's goals seems to be to offer a balanced portrayal of both white and black perspectives without condemning either side. Does the novel succeed in this goal? Is it too judgmental? Does it oversimplify any issues?

2. In some ways, *Cry, the Beloved Country* seems to be a novel designed to convince South African society of the value of equality and social justice. What methods does it use to do so? Are some more effective than others?

3. Both Kumalo and Jarvis undergo revelations during the novel. Jarvis finally sees the injustice of South African society, and Kumalo realizes the consequences of losing the old tribal customs. Compare the two men's journeys over the course of the novel. In what ways are they alike? In what ways do they differ?

4. What role do women play in the novel? How do the injustices they face affect them? Do they suffer from injustices that the men do not?

5. *Cry, the Beloved Country* contrasts the rural and urban ways of life. How do the world of Johannesburg and the world of Ndotsheni differ? Does one place seem to be more just than the other? Does one place seem more likely to produce a just South Africa?

Review & Resources

Quiz

1. Which of the following men is not a priest?

    A. Msimangu
    B. Father Vincent
    C. Mr. Carmichael
    D. Kumalo

2. Whom does Kumalo bring from Johannesburg to Ndotsheni?

    A. Msimangu and Mrs. Lithebe
    B. Absalom's wife and Gertrude's son
    C. Absalom and Gertrude
    D. Jarvis and his grandson

3. What money does Kumalo use for his trip to Johannesburg?

    A. The money he and his wife have been saving for Absalom's schooling
    B. The money he has been saving to build a new church
    C. Money given to him by Msimangu
    D. Money given to him by Jarvis

4. What happens to Gertrude at the end of the novel?

    A. She becomes a nun
    B. She returns to prostitution
    C. She gets married
    D. She disappears

5. Who is John Harrison?

    A. Jarvis's nephew
    B. Mary's husband
    C. Arthur's brother-in-law
    D. Jarvis's grandson

6. Why don't black mine workers bring their families
    to Johannesburg?

    A.   Their families prefer to stay in the rural villages
    B.   The mine workers prefer to live alone
    C.   There is no housing for the families
    D.   Johannesburg is too dangerous for wives and children

7. What happens when the police catch Absalom?

    A.   He makes a desperate effort to escape
    B.   He confesses everything
    C.   He attempts to harm himself
    D.   He writes to his father

8. Who comes to visit Kumalo and practice his Zulu?

    A.   Arthur's son
    B.   Jarvis's son
    C.   John Harrison
    D.   Gertrude's son

9. Who is pregnant when the novel ends?

    A.   Mary Jarvis
    B.   Gertrude
    C.   Mrs. Kumalo
    D.   Absalom's wife

10. What happens in the church in Ndotsheni during
    the confirmation?

    A.   Part of the roof falls in
    B.   The roof leaks rain
    C.   A little girl runs out crying
    D.   Arthur's son runs in screaming

11. Why are the village children dying?

    A.   They lack milk
    B.   They lack bread
    C.   They lack medicine
    D.   They lack juice

12. What is the topic of John's speech, to which Kumalo and
    Jarvis listen?

    A.   The need for a violent uprising against the whites
    B.   The need for new schools for the children
    C.   The rights of black South Africans to vote
    D.   The need for higher wages for black miners

13. Who dies on confirmation day in Ndotsheni?

    A.   Absalom
    B.   Margaret Jarvis
    C.   The Bishop
    D.   Mrs. Kumalo

14. What does *umfundisi* mean?

    A.   "White person"
    B.   "Sir"
    C.   "Parson"
    D.   "Judge"

15. Why does Kumalo go up into the mountain?

    A.   To ponder how to help Ndotsheni
    B.   To await Absalom's execution
    C.   To meet Jarvis
    D.   To exercise

16. What does the novel say is the basis of
    Johannesburg's wealth?

    A.   Gold
    B.   Copper
    C.   Oil
    D.   Silver

17. Why was Absalom at the reformatory?

    A.   He had gotten a girl pregnant
    B.   He had attempted to kill a man
    C.   He was in trouble for his political views
    D.   He was in trouble for stealing

18.   Where are Absalom and Kumalo finally reunited?

A.   At the Mission House
B.   At the prison
C.   In the courtroom
D.   In Shanty Town

19.   What weapon does Johannes carry when the boys try to rob Arthur Jarvis?

A.   A gun
B.   A knife
C.   An iron rod
D.   A wooden stick

20.   Other than his politics, how does John Kumalo make his living?

A.   He is a lawyer
B.   He is a farmer
C.   He is a carpenter
D.   He is a teacher

21.   Why did Absalom's wife run away from her home?

A.   She fought with her brothers
B.   Her mother drank too much and she did not get along with her stepfather
C.   She was pregnant
D.   She wanted to work

22.   Who gives Msimangu and Kumalo a ride to Alexandra?

A.   A white driver
B.   A black driver
C.   The police
D.   John Kumalo

23.   What is the chief's role in building the dam?

A.   He is the engineer
B.   He is paying for it
C.   He has no role
D.   He is in charge of guarding the flags

REVIEW & RESOURCES

24. Which priest marries Absalom and his girlfriend?

   A. Kumalo
   B. Msimangu
   C. Johannes Pafuri
   D. Father Vincent

25. Who orchestrates the building of Shanty Town?

   A. John Kumalo
   B. Tomlinson
   C. Dubula
   D. Arthur Jarvis

ANSWER KEY:
1: C; 2: B; 3: A; 4: D; 5: C; 6: C; 7: B; 8: A; 9: D; 10: B; 11:
A; 12: D; 13: B; 14: C; 15: B; 16: A; 17: D; 18: B; 19: C; 20:
C; 21: B; 22: A; 23: D; 24: D; 25: C

SUGGESTIONS FOR FURTHER READING

ALEXANDER, PETER. *Alan Paton: A Biography.* New York: Oxford University Press, 1994.

ATTRIDGE, DEREK, and ROSEMARY JOLLY, eds. *Writing South Africa: Literature, Apartheid, and Democracy, 1970–1995.* Cambridge University Press, 1998.

BAKER, SHERIDAN, ed. *Paton's* CRY, THE BELOVED COUNTRY: *The Novel, the Critics, the Setting.* New York: Charles Scribner's Sons, 1968.

BONNER, PHILIP, DEBORAH POSEL, PETER DELIUS, eds. *Apartheid's Genesis, 1935–1962.* Johannesburg: Ravan Press, 1994.

CALLAN, EDWARD. *Cry, the Beloved Country: A Novel of South Africa.* Boston: Twayne Publishers, 1991.

———. *Alan Paton.* Boston: Twayne Publishers, 1982.

SPARKS, ALLISTER. *The Mind of South Africa.* New York: Alfred A. Knopf, 1990.

REVIEW & RESOURCES

SparkNotes Study Guides: